HUMANITY'S SEARCH FOR THE MEANING OF LIFE

A Brief Survey of History, Philosophy, Religion,
Art, Music, and Architecture

THIRD EDITION

June Stephenson, Ph.D.

Diemer, Smith Publlishing Company, Inc.

Other Books by June Stephenson

The Administrator
It's All Right to Get Old
Women's Roots
A Lie is a Debt
Womankind
Innocent Weapons
Male Crime in America
Sticks and Stones are the Easy Part
Poisonous Power: Childhood Roots of Tyranny

Dedicated to my husband

WILLIAM OTTO BUEHLER

with appreciation for his great faith in me.

Acknowledgments

To the thousands of people who have already purchased this book, *Humanity's Search for the Meaning of Life*, I sincerely thank you and acknowledge that your purchases and letters have been the encouragement for me to write this third edition.

To my family and friends who are always supportive of my writing, I express my gratitude now, which I may not have done already.

To my good friend, Margaret Paul, who proofed this manuscript as well as the manuscript for the second edition, I thank you for standing by with patience and pencil.

To my computer tutor, Garry Carter, who taught me how to use Microsoft Word and Ventura Publisher software programs to typeset this manuscript, I thank you for your skill and endurance.

CONTENTS

Introduction

Throughout the whole of history, people have searched for the meaning of their lives, leaving a rich accumulation of writings, philosophies, dramas, religions, paintings, sculptures, buildings and music. These creative expressions affirmed life for some people, somewhere, at some time. Every creation around you which is made by a human being represents someone's humanity. The chair you're sitting in, the clothes you're wearing, the building you're in, or your home, even the time of day which people created, all are representative of someone's humanity -- their human-ness. In other words, everything that human beings have created can be classified as part of the humanities.

More specifically, though, the humanities usually refer to the Fine Arts, which include painting, sculpture, and music. We will be concerned here with these Fine Arts, and also with the intellectual and theological realms of literature, philosophy, and religion. As architecture is said to be the "stage-setting" for our personalities, and as architecture reflects a culture's strivings, a short history of building design concludes this book.

Chapter One provides a brief look at the history of men and women in western civilization. It is important in any study of creativity to know a little about the world at the time the object originated, or the ideas were first expressed. For instance, it is good to know why the art form of the Medieval period was predominantly of religious subjects, and why modern art is abstract, why the musical scores that were written in the Romantic period were heavy with sweet melodies, and why today's musical creations often submerge the melody in preference for loud rhythm. All of this is leading to the premise that a short history of people on earth is necessary for an understanding of why people created what they did.

Chapter Two is an introduction to philosophy, with a review of questions that have been with us since people first began to record their thoughts. These questions, still with us today, include, "Why are we alive?" "What is love?" "What is justice?" "What is one's purpose on earth?" "Are people created equal?" This philosophy section includes a short discussion of the lives and works of several famous philosophers who lived from 1000 B.C., to the present.

Chapter Three introduces religion as a social institution which people seemed to have needed and have relied upon in every community and in every time-period. The precepts of five major religions of the world are briefly summarized. These include Hinduism, Buddhism, Judaism, Christianity, and Islam.

Chapter Four is a history of pictorial art from "primitive" cave paintings to modern abstract expressionism and surrealism, with pictorial examples from each time-period.

Chapter Five is a history of music, with a brief discussion of some famous composers and a list of famous musicians throughout history.

Chapter Six is a history of architecture, with a few select pictorial examples of architectural styles of particular time-periods.

In each section, whether the discussion is philosophy, religion, or any of the Fine Arts, these will be related to the times in which their styles flourished. The author hopes that this book will provide a continuity in history and an understanding of artistic creations and intellectual development that will help the reader relate his or her own world to the whole human endeavor on earth. It is hoped also that this book will help people become more tolerant of others whose art is different from theirs, whose music is not their style, and whole philosophy and religion are different from their own. If people expand their understanding of others, this understanding can't help but ease the strife, however slightly, in a world torn with political, racial, and religious conflicts.

Chapter One

THE HISTORY OF HUMAN BEINGS

The major periods in history are divided into five lengths of time. Historians may disagree with these dates, but for the purpose of this book we will relate to the following years and historical periods:

Prehistory ...... 550,000 B.C. to 2500 B.C.
Antiquity .... 2,500 B.C. to 400 A.D.
Medieval ....400 A.D. to 1400 A.D.
Renaissance ...... 1,400 A.D. to 1700 A.D.
Modern .... 1,700 A.D. to present.

It is necessary to differentiate between "B.C." and "A.D." which a time-line makes clear. Though not accurate definition of the terms, "A.D." and B.C." it may be easier to remember if one thinks of "B.C." as years "Before Christ," and the years "A.D." as the years "After Christ's Death." The time-line will help, denoting the Birth of Christ as the separation of

Time — Line

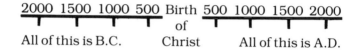

| 2000 1500 1000 500 | Birth of Christ | 500 1000 1500 2000 |
| All of this is B.C. | | All of this is A.D. |

"Before," and "After," henceforth referred to as "B.C." and "A.D."

PREHISTORIC PERIOD

550,000 B.C. to 2500 B.C.

This is the period marking the first evidence of human existence up until the time that people began to purposefully leave a definite record of themselves. "pre," means "before," Therefore prehistoric means "before history."

The Biblical theory in Genesis is one of the many theories concerning human beginning on earth. Each religion makes a statement about the origins of humans on earth, which religious people accept as faith. There is no controversy in this text as to which theory is "the truth." The scientific theory, also just a theory, filled with conjecture and probabilities, will be discussed here in this history section.

Pithecanthropus Erectus

The scientific theory suggests that a sub-human appeared as an erect creature probably around 500,000 B.C. and was much later given the name of Pithecanthropus Erectus. The National Geographic Public Broadcast of April, 1988, informed us that the human element appeared even earlier, in Tanzania, and that recently a complete skeleton of a twelve year old boy was found, dating back to more than a million and a half years ago.

The skeletal fossil remains of Pithecanthropus indicate a flat forehead, flat cranial roof and massive protruding jaws, differing considerably from Homo Sapiens, the term identifying modern humans. The limbs of Pithecanthropus are the same as Homo Sapiens, indicating that the brain and skull developed much later than limbs.

Pithecanthropus

Artist's Conception of Pithecanthropus Erectus

Because of the situation in which the fossils of Pithecanthropus were discovered in Java and in China, it is known that they were cave dwellers and hunters and gatherers. They had simple stone implements and used fire for cooking. The tools which people use indicate their behavior. Flakes from rocks were chipped to produce razor sharp implements, good for butchering animals. This indicated thoughtful foresight and planning. As the marrow in animals is nutritious because it is high in calories and in fat, prehistoric men used heavy axe-like tools to crack animal bones.

A question is often asked at this point in a discussion of early human beings, "How are we different from animals?" Bronowski, who wrote *The Ascent of Man*, says, other than the fact that we can oppose the thumb and forefinger, we also have speech. And if we are any kind of a machine, we are a learning machine. But the central thing, he says, is the ability to plan action a long way off for which the reward is a long way off.

Neanderthal

It wasn't until about 50,000 B.C. that another sub-human appeared, referred to as Neanderthal. Neanderthal Man is said to have developed after the fourth ice age. For hundreds of thousands of year in this prehistoric period it is calculated that there were four ice ages. There are several theories about how the ice ages started and why the earth thawed only to freeze over again four times.

Fossils of Neanderthal men and women, discovered in 1856 in Neander Valley, Germany, have thick skulls and massive, chinless jaws like Pithecanthropus. But unlike Pithecanthropus and modern men and women, Neanderthals have very large brains -- larger than our own. The common misconception of Neanderthals as brutish, stupid people is very likely erroneous. The question of why such large brains were needed may be answered by considering what the Neanderthal had to contend with to survive. They lived in difficult climactic times as the glaciers receded. They fought mammoth rhinoceroses and bears with crude stone axes and they needed all their wits to survive. It may be that as we turn over our calculations for survival to mechanization, robots and computers, our brains will decrease in size.

Neanderthal Man

It is interesting to note that Neanderthals were the first known humans to bury their dead, which links them to us. The remains of Neanderthals have been discovered in many parts of the world though we don't know where they came from or why they disappeared. In Israel, an excavation of a

Neanderthal camp, which produced thousands of tools and many skeletons, was begun thirty years ago and will continue for many more years. As anthropology is only about one hundred years old, our technologies for unearthing the past are not fully developed. We will never fully excavate a "digs," because scientists who come later will have better tools

Cro Magnon

In 1868, in France, the first skeleton of a Cro Magnon man was discovered. The skeleton was

Artist's Conception of Cro-Magnon

about 30,000 years old and looked very much as our skeletons look now. Cro Magnon lived from about 35,000 to 10,000 years ago. From their living quarters we know that Cro Magnons used more elaborate tools than Pithecanthropus Erectus or Neanderthals. They used spear throwers and probably the bow and arrow. Bone and ivory were engraved for artistic ornaments and the cave paintings of animals which date from about 15,000 B.C. are attributed to Cro Magnon or Early Homo Sapiens of the Neolithic period, which is the geological period of our time. There are differing theories about these cave drawings, which will be discussed more fully in the History of Art section of this book. It is generally believed that though some of these drawings may have been created by the Cro-Magnons, most were probably created about 15,000 B.C. by Neolithic people whose presence was first recorded by these cave drawings at that time.

Hunters and Gatherers

During this long period of time, life style was most probably nomadic. The men were the hunters of animals for food and the women and children the gatherers of fruits and nuts and roots which were edible. People lived where they could find food, and the weather being icy cold, food was not plentiful.

Referring to the book, *The Paleolithic Experience,* the authors stress that hunting on foot and gathering food for long hours built the stamina of the prehistoric people. Also, compared to our modern diet, the early diet was more healthful. "Sitting at a desk, buttering bread and gaining weight has little survival value," one of the authors, Melvin Konner, stated at an American Association for the Advancement of Science meeting.

After studying the Kung San tribe in Botswana and Zambia, Konner said that the nursing habits of Kung women and presumably of all hunters and gatherers have set a natural sort of family planning. Women nurse their babies about four times an hour for about four years, then the children stop drinking milk altogether. Nursing for so many years means that the children are spaced at least about four years apart because frequent nursing stimulates the hormone which acts to prevent conception. The Kung do not use artificial contraception, but the nursing process is a kind of natural population control. As the population is kept low, people live in harmony with their environment and do not need to kill off animals to extinction, or decimate the plant life. The importance of studying a tribe like this is to relate what we learn about hunters and gatherers today to those of thousands of years ago.

Age of Cultivation

It is with the Neolithic people that tremendous changes in life styles are thought to have taken place. In approximately 15,000 B.C. THE AGE OF CULTIVATION began. What vastly different changes would cultivating the soil have on people who had been nomadic, moving from place to place to find food? Most likely as soon as they learned to manipulate their environment to plant seeds and harvest crops they were freed from the necessity of moving on and on to find food supplies.

But why did this all take place around 15,000 B.C? Why not sooner? What was there around 15,000 B.C. that was different from the thousands of years before, that encouraged people to plant seeds and stay around the area long enough to harvest and eat the fruits of their labor?

Much of what we know is conjecture, but scientists say that the fourth ice age was well over by 15,000 B.C. and the world was warming up so that things could grow more easily. But even at that, why did people start to plant food? What gave them the idea when it had not been their way of life before?

One of the more interesting theories comes from the legends related to burial and sacrifice. It is theorized that when prehistoric people buried their dead, they left the deceased person some implements and grain for the next life. If an animal were slaughtered to be placed with the body, the blood's moisture nourished the grain and the grain sprouted at some later time. People may have related the growth of the grain with the death of a person, or the blood of an animal, or both. And this is where the idea of making sacrifice is said to have begun. People might have felt that if crops were to grow, possibly blood was necessary for plant growth.

After people had put grain in the ground and related that process to the food for the future, they could stay in one place and eat their crops as the crops matured. It is believed that this happened first in three river valleys -- the fertile valleys of the Nile River, the Tigres-Euphrates, and the Indus River where three or four crops a year could be raised. It follows that with the AGE OF CULTIVATION people first began to learn about the seasons.

From Families to Tribes

As the earth warmed up, more and more people moved into the rich, fertile river delta areas. They joined others for their mutual food raising, for defense, and for sacrifice. Eventually they formed into tribes -- the first large and more permanent groups of people staying in one area for long periods of time, if not for their life-time.

The social hierarchy developed from the family, which was a woman and her children, to kinship groups, to the clan, then to tribes, and finally to nations. The first families were unlike what are referred to as "nuclear families" or "natural families" today. In prehistoric times as fatherhood was unknown, women were worshipped as supernatural beings because they could bring human life into existence. It was believed that a woman became pregnant because she walked in a lagoon at a certain time of the evening when the moon was at a specific height, for instance, or that she passed by a certain tree in the jungle. The relationship between sexual intercourse and human reproduction was not surmised until the domestication of animals, when the male's role was established. Until it was determined that men had a part in the birth of children, all children belonged to the mother. The principal man in a child's life was the child's mother's brother, or uncle.

The Supernatural

Leaders naturally evolved in these large groups of people. These were usually the most clever people -- those who could predict the weather, or provide herbal cures for illness. As wisdom gives a person a certain measure of control, these leaders became the first political leaders, known as SHAMAN or PRIESTESSES or PRIESTS. People looked to them for help and guidance. These who could predict the weather were thought to be able to CONTROL it. They were credited with supernatural power. With these priests or priestesses or Shaman, with the ritual of sacrifice, and the dependence on the seasons for food, the beginnings of religion, or worship, or fear of the supernatural began.

Beginnings of the Spoken Word

As tribes stayed together through the generations, they developed some method of verbal recording of the trials and triumphs of the tribe. People who knew each other well, used the same sounds and gestures to communicate. Each family joining the tribe had its own sounds and gestures. As tribes grew in size, absorbing more people, they needed to agree on sound and gesture so that all would know what was being communicated. In this way, human beings advanced from being relatively nonverbal to being capable of actual words. THE AGE OF CULTIVATION brought the beginnings of the spoken word.

The Bard

The history of the tribe was verbally recorded and passed on by a particular person in the group with an excellent memory and a good voice. Eventually this tribal history was sung and phrased in rhyme to be repeated and learned more easily. the person responsible for this method of communicating and recording history was called a BARD This style of recording history later became known as EPIC POETRY. These are the long poetic sagas of conquests, loves, arguments, and victories that were memorized and repeated over and over again. As there was yet no written language, the young children of the tribe "learned their lessons," by hearing the history of the tribe repeated over and over again. History lessons which are rhymed and sung are much easier to memorize than pages such as these.

Stone Age - 10,000 B.C.

Let's go now to what is known as THE STONE AGE, which began about 10,000 B.C.and is known for the stone implements, bone needles with eyes, and barbed spearheads. There are several tribes today living in a STONE AGE culture who have never evolved to the point where they use metal. The Tasaday Indians in the Philippine Islands are such a tribe, discovered recently, living in a remote jungle area, completely self-sufficient. Explorations into their territory found them living as people lived about 10,000 B.C. When they were discovered, they had no metal implements. They live from day to day, the men hunting for animals and fish to eat, and the women and children occupied with gathering food, which means picking fruits or nuts or other jungle edibles. Though some people have said that the Tasaday are a hoax, that they were never were a typical Stone Age tribe, others claim that they could not have been trained to speak a different language or to maintain a "phoney" life style for 18 years.

Other tribes of Stone Age cultures existing today include the Australian Aborigines, some of the Caribou Eskimos, tribes in South America and Africa. Some of these tribes do not even use the bow and arrow.

It has been suggested that the diet of our stone age ancestors was more healthful than our diets today. Stone age men and women ate wild game, plants, nuts and roots. They ate a lot of meat, but it was much leaner than the meat of today because they ate animals that had been active, not animals that had been raised in confined areas, fattened for profit. The authors of the book, *The Paleolithic Experience*, suggest that our bodies have not changed much since the stone age, but our diets have. We are therefore more prone to diseases of civilization, such as diabetes, cancer, heart disease, and hypertension which prehistoric people did not have. However, we cannot dismiss the fact that our life span is far greater than theirs because of other health improvements.

In a recent excavation in Titusville, Florida, in 1984, 125 skeletons, wrapped in fine cloth and buried for eight thousand years in a peat bog, were unearthed. The brains of 91 of these Indians were preserved enough for microbiologists to extract the DNA. A recognizable genetic message was found corresponding to a gene in modern people. From these brains it may be possible to discover family relationships in a vanished people.

The skeletons are of men, women, and children and are believed to be a band of hunters and gatherers. It was also discovered that many of the skeletons had broken bones which might indicate they were a violent people. An antler shaped into a spear point was found in one skeleton's hip bone, and nearly all skeletons had indications of joint disease. Also, for the first time, antibodies were found in excavated skeletons, though none of the type made by the immune system to fight tooth-decay bacteria. It is thought, therefore, that these people had no tooth decay. Examining the bones for carbon and nitrogen, the anthropologists concluded that these hunters and gatherers were heavy seafood eaters.

Bronze Age - 3500 B.C. to 1800 B.C.

The dates of the Bronze Age differ depending on which region of the world is being considered. The dates from 2000 B.C. to 1800 B.C. are the dates for the Bronze Age in Europe. In any place, the Bronze Age is the period between the Stone Age and the Iron Age, depending on what those dates are in the locality considered. The Bronze Age is so named because of the use of bronze, which is a metal derived from combining copper and tin. Often the objects from the Bronze Age are of Oriental patterns and designs, indicating the Eastern beginnings of this age. This age is also associated with cremation of the dead, rather than internment in the earth.

These early ages are the beginnings of the time when human beings attempt to control their environment, unlike the animals which survive in spite of the environment. But as human beings learn to control their environment by making tools, such as stone implements, and bronze tools, we also learn to destroy our environment by making automobiles which emit poisonous exhaust into the air we breathe. We also have learned to use chemicals which become toxic waste polluting our drinking water and food supply.

Iron Age

The Iron Age began about 1000 B.C. by people known as Urnfield invaders, who settled in Central Europe after migrating north from Greece and Italy. They brought with them their knowledge of iron metallurgy which they had acquired from their neighbors to the south. The Urnfields, as early as 700 B.C., had two-wheeled chariots and they could work in sheet metal.

In Summary

Age of Cultivation 15,000 B.C.
Stone Age ...... 10,000 B.C.
Bronze Age .... 3,500 B.C.
Iron Age .... 1,000 B.C.

Early Dynastic Period - 5000 B.C.

What has been developed in these early ages was further developed by tribes in the Early Dynastic Period in Egypt around 5000 B.C. Various tribes had settled into villages, used metal instruments, and perfected the making of pottery. The Priests, who now called themselves Pharaohs, gave themselves further supernatural powers and called themselves God, or God-King.

In the Early Dynastic Period there is evidence of the domestication of animals, the use of the wheel, the use of the chariot with the horse, which meant that fights between tribes could be more mobile, that one tribe could invade the villages of another at a greater distance and bring slaves back home to do their menial labor.

There is evidence, in this period, too, of some writing, some arithmetic and geometry, some art, and the beginning of architectural structures which are more than grass huts. And since there were the bow and arrow, there is supposition that stringed instruments existed.

Use of Money

It is the existence of the use of money in this time that tells us there was the beginning of a complex society. Some sort of barter is always with us, exchanging one thing for another, but when a standardized value is put on pieces of metal to be worth an agreed-upon number of things, then society has gone beyond its initial stage.

Domestication of the Horse

Once, also, that the horse was domesticated and the chariot invented, society was indeed out of its early stage, and strategic warfare was ever-after a part of the human scene. Men could now travel great distances to conquer enemies, bring back slaves and treasure, and expand their own territories. As Robert O'Connell writes in his book, *Of Arms and Men*, " ...women were excluded from... virtually all ...forms of organized combat...warfare preserved the role of the female as prize and object of combat."

Warfare with horses attached to chariots, and soldiers shooting arrows from bows from the chariots was limited. Sometime around 875 B.C. soldiers mounted horses and rode them into combat. Archers on horseback in Assyria are pictured without saddles and, therefore, also without stirrups. What a precarious position from which to aim an arrow! While the stirrup was probably first used by the Mongolians in Central Asia around 600 A.D., it would be several hundred years later before it was used in the Western world, making possible the Knight on horseback.

The Medieval Knight, wearing his suit of metal, dominated the battlefield for 500 years, but disappeared with the invention of gun powder. Though horses have been used in armies even in recent times, they cannot compete with armored tanks and are now used almost entirely for ceremonial activities.

Beginnings of Civilization

All of the preceding has been leading up to the advent of what is termed "civilization." H.G.Wells in his *Outline of History* has said that there are three things necessary for the existence of civilization:

1.People settle continuously where they cultivate.
2.They live in buildings continuously.
3.They have rules that all are expected to live by.

Western Civilization began in approximately 2500 B.C. in the area near the mouth of the Tigres-Euphrates River in what is now Iraq. Here the people developed the City of UR in the area called SUMER. They left a variety of artistic objects which tell us about their lives. Items of trade from India have been found in the ruins of Sumer which indicate the Eastern Civilization was also well on its way at the same time as Western Civilization. There have been products made in Sumer which have been found in the ancient ruins of India and China, which further tell us that trade between the East and West has been going on since the dawn of history.

So we have come down to the dawn of history because it is at Sumer that PRE-history ends and history begins. From now on, people made a conscientious effort to record their story. In a multitude of ways they tell us something about their search for the meaning of their lives. We have moved from the long, long prehistoric period into the age of ANTIQ-UITY, also known as the ANCIENT, or CLASSI-CAL PERIOD, which began about 2500 B.C.

ANTIQUITY

2500 B.C. to 400 A.D.

Civilizations emerged in this order:

Persia

Egypt

Greece

Rome

Persians

As you know, civilization does not just one day blossom on the plains of history. It was many thousands of years in the coming, gradually evolving through the tribes into the settled communities. Sumer, which was in ancient Mesopotamia, later called Persia, included the city states of Nippur, Ur, Lagash, Urak, Khafajah, and Kish.

In the periods between 4500 and 2400 B.C. the Sumerians imported metals from Turkey, developed the first known written language, made jewels and weapons, and expanded trade.

Cuneiform, which means wedge shaped, were marks which became the writing form. This writing was adopted by the Assyrians and the Babylonians, but the Egyptians developed a different method. Pressed into clay, these cuneiform tablets have become permanent records which tell us about the life in Sumer long, long ago.

The tablet on the left in this picture is almost 5000 years old. It is thought to be a bookkeeping record while the tablet on the right is thought to be a record of division of land.

Sumerian is the oldest known written language. About one million clay tablets have been excavated, the first by archaeologists in 1887. But perhaps 100 million more clay tablets still lie buried. University of Pennsylvania researchers have been translating a Sumerian dictionary since 1976 which they say may take them fifty years to complete.

Civilization travels by one or two methods: by war or by trade. People in one area who want to own the artifacts or spices or other things from another area have two choices. They can steal the products through warfare, and at the same time bring back captives to do their menial work, or they can open up trade routes and use an agreed-upon money value. Regardless of which method is used, knowledge and life styles are often exchanged from one group to another. What one community knows, the other has access to. The Sumerians left evidence of credit systems and some complicated system of justice, both dependent upon the knowledge of writing.

And in everything there were gods. Not only were there universal gods, but there were also city gods. Massive temples were built which were the hub of business as well as religious life. So much gold and silver ornamentation has been unearthed that it is reasonable to assume that Sumer was exceedingly rich.

It was recorded that in Sumer, slaves could own land, even buy their freedom, though they were also flogged. Eventually the city states of Sumer were taken over by the Babylonians. The law code of Hammurabi, the first great king of Babylon, is today's evidence that the Babylonians were ruled by many laws which dated back to Sumer.

Egyptians

By 1800 B.C., Sumer had perished, coming under the influence of Babylonian domination. But before Sumer fell, the peoples who lived in Egypt had traded with those in Sumer, in what is now Iraq. The Egyptians brought back the art forms from Sumer, and they also brought back ideas of government. The Egyptians were the next people to emerge with a civilization. They took the meager writings of the Sumerians and made the alphabet, which was a significant contribution to humanity. They also had earlier developed the idea of the "God-Kings," an idea which came right down through history until the French Revolution, known at that later time as "The Divine Right of Kings."

The Egyptians invented paper and ink and the world's first calendar of 365 days. Their civilization, lasting from 2700 B.C. until the period shortly after the Birth of Christ, is divided into three Kingdoms, known as Old, Middle, and New, through 30 ruling families or Dynasties, until the last founded by Ptolemy in 320 B.C.

The Egyptians were masters of stone work that we see still standing. They used almost no metal and they had no animals. Their belief in immortality was coupled with their desire for massiveness as we see today in their pyramids. Their art was centered on religion which was associated with the after-life. Statues are stiff, rather squared, and motionless in appearance. They believed in many gods, although Amenhotep IV tried to persuade his people to believe in one god whom he called Aton. But even with Queen Nefertiti's efforts against pantheism (belief in many gods) Amenhotep's efforts to change the religion of Egypt failed.

Egypt was invaded in turn by Ethiopians, Babylonians, Assyrians, Persians, and finally in 330 B.C. by the Greek, Alexander the Great.

Phoenicians

The Phoenicians, who lived on the coast of the Mediterranean Sea, and traveled extensively around the Mediterranean area were known as "the middlemen of civilization." Their excellent ship-building talents were in demand in the Mediterranean area. The goods produced in one country were transported by the Phoenicians into the other countries, along with Phoenician skills in metallurgy. They improved on the Egyptian alphabet, incorporating a system of sounds which we refer to today as phonetics.

As their trade expanded, they set up many cities around the Mediterranean, the one most powerful being the city of Carthage. From this strong city the Phoenicians challenged the Greeks who acquired much of their culture henceforth from the Phoenicians and later transmitted it to the Romans.

Greeks

Thus, from the first civilization in Sumer in 2500 B.C., civilization inched its way along the coast of Egypt and across the Mediterranean Sea. And 1500 years later the Greek civilization began.

The Greek Bard, Homer, is believed to have lived around 1000 B.C., though his long epic poems, *"The Iliad"* and *"The Odyssey"* were not written down until about 500 B.C. *"The Iliad,"* one of the first pieces of recorded literature, describes important events in a long war. Professional poets, or Bards, passed this history along, orally, for hundreds of years until it could be written. *"The Odyssey"* is the story of a man trying to return home from war. Here is a short section of the beginning of this epic poem attributed to Homer.

Sing in me, Muse, and through me tell the story of that man skilled in all ways of contending, the wanderer, harried for years on end, after he plundered the stronghold on the proud height of Troy.

He saw the townlands and learned the minds of many distant men, and weathered many bitter nights and days in his deep heart at sea, while he fought only to save his life, to bring his shipmates home. But not by will nor valor could he save them, for their own recklessness destroyed them all -- children and fools, they killed and feasted on the cattle of Lord Helios, the Sun, and he who moves all day through heaven took from their eyes the dawn of their return.

Of these adventures, Muse, daughter of Zeus, tell us in our time, lift the great song again. Begin when all the rest who left behind them headlong death in a battle or at sea had long ago returned, while he alone still hungered for home and wife. Her ladyship Kalypso clung to him in her sea-hollowed caves- a nymph, immortal and most beautiful, who craved him for her own.

And when long years and seasons Wheeling brought around that point of time ordained for him to make his passage homeward, trials and dangers, even so, attended him even in Ithaka, near those he loved. Yet all the gods had pitied Lord Odysseus, all but Poseidon, raging cold and rough against the brave king till he came ashore at last on his own land.

Though recited aloud for hundreds of years, the epic poetry of Homer was finally written down during what is known as the GOLDEN AGE OF GREECE, an historical period around 500 B.C. This was a period, abundant in art, architecture, philosophy, and what could be termed today, modern ideas on government. The GOLDEN AGE OF GREECE gave to the history of philosophy such names as Socrates, Plato and Aristotle. It left a wealth of Greek drama which students have studied almost continuously to this day. Greek civilization was unique in that all art forms were sponsored by the government, giving the Greeks great civic pride.

After hundreds of years and many wars between the city-states of Greece, the energy of that country lay wasted. The glory of Greece came to an end at about the same time that Rome was blossoming.

Romans

A great deal of the cultural civilization of Rome was achieved by copying from the Greeks. Even their famous epic poem, "*The Aeneid*," by Virgil, is based on the poetic form of the Greek Homer's "*Iliad*," and "*Odyssey*."

Roman contribution to culture in western civilization is not as much in art as it is in other things such as their systematizing of the law, and their network of roads which are still used to this day.

The Roman's significant contribution to the world of art is in their use of the Italian marble, especially in the carving of statues of their leaders. These were representational carvings of the shoulders and head and were referred to as "busts," at that time, a new rendition in the history of art.

As each of the preceding civilizations had deteriorated and eventually collapsed, other civilizations elsewhere had grown to power, flourished, and then collapsed to be superceded by yet another civilization. But with the collapse of Rome, western civilization itself virtually disappeared.

Remember that we are talking about Western Civilization. Eastern Civilization of the Orient, India, China, had a different experience.

Their civilizations continued, though their glory and power dissipated in some areas and under some leaders and rose yet again in other places and under other leaders. But in Eastern Civilization there is a continuity that is not evident in Western Civilization. And because civilization almost disappeared from our heritage, the study of the Fall of Rome has occupied historians ever since the threads of civilization were picked up again hundreds of years after the collapse.

What caused the fall of Rome? Since other civilizations had been emerging one after another for about 3000 years, why did this process cease in the West for approximately 1000 years? Gibbon has written many volumes on the fall of Rome, and other historians have written the subject into the ground. So to attempt an easy analysis here is presumptuous. Nevertheless a summary of a few reasons often projected as the causes of the fall of Rome follows:

1. The government extended its forces too far and provided little "home rule" in the conquered territories.
2. There were too many excesses -- human sacrifices were for "fun and games."
3. There were not enough rewards for being a good Roman as compared to the rewards offered by the new religion, Christianity. For a government to last it has to offer both rewards and punishments. Roman government provided too many punishments compared to Christianity which did not punish in this life. Christianity offered the reward of Everlasting Life After Death. That was

better than anything the Romans had to offer and it made suffering in life on earth tolerable for the Christians.

4. There were too many extremes between rich and poor. When this happens it often opens the way for invaders or general disruption. The Roman Empire was ripe for destruction.

5. There was no "culture" of Roman origin. Their art and architecture, their music and their style of literature had all been borrowed from the Greeks. They, therefore, lacked a national pride to "rally around," and defend.

The complete fall of Rome took about two hundred years. Tribes from the northern part of the European continent began sweeping down on the Roman-occupied areas and were joined by the dissatisfied peasants who had suffered under Roman rule. There was a general disintegration of the quality of Roman life. When the famous aqueducts had been cut by the Barbarian hordes from the north, this meant that the rich Romans could no longer live comfortably up on their hill palaces, but had to draw their water from the Tiber River down along the banks with the poor people.

Disease was having its day. There were four great epidemics of the plague which left cities practically vacant. The Bubonic plague (also known as The Black Death), of 524, reduced the population of Europe almost as severly as the Black Death of the 1500's. The fear of barbarians, the fear of a killing disease and depopulated cities, caused commerce to come to a virtual halt.

With the eventual arrival of the tribes known as Barbarians, Rome collapsed. Everything changed -- the most dramatic being the change in the school system where there was complete disintegration. After the collapse of the Empire, the newly emerging Christian Church took responsibility for whatever education there was.

The great civilizations were exhausted and what there was on the Western continent was not in any way organized. It was a feuding group of areas that did not emerge as cities of importance for several hundreds of years. With the fall of Rome, civilization as it had been known in the Western world, disappeared for about one thousand years.

MEDIEVAL PERIOD

400 A.D. to 1400 A.D.

What was going on in those years from 400 to 1400 A.D. known as the Medieval Period or the Middle Ages? And why is this period also known as the Dark Ages? What was "Dark" about this period?

We know that the collapse of the Roman Empire destroyed the educational system within the empire, and the "Light of Learning" barely glimmered in the western world. Over the hundreds of years, whatever written knowledge did manage to survive, was contained in three or four written manuscripts by Latin authors. These were carried by a few Christian monks across Europe and then across the waters to an unlikely place in Western Ireland. There, western civilization took a "toe hold" and held on.

Monks in the Monasteries

In 500 A.D. about fifty scholars who had arrived in Cork, Ireland, set to copying, recopying and studying their few manuscripts of ancient writing which they had brought with them from the European continent. These were writings of the classical writers of the ancient world-- writing which had survived hundreds of years and had been carefully protected through the ravages of war and plunder. The monks who had come to remote Cork, Ireland, brought with them the first monastic society and they settled into a kind of permanence which is necessary for a civilization.

Now and then they were grossly intruded upon by the Vikings from the north, but in spite of this, the monks maintained a settlement and kept at their scholarly work. "The Light of Learning" continued to glow, if only very dimly, in those early years of the Medieval Period, in a cold, northern part of the western world.

Charlemagne

If there are any two things which could be credited with saving western civilization after the fall of Rome, it would be (1) the monks in the monasteries who learned and copied the ancient texts and thereby kept knowledge alive, and (2) a man who ruled what is now much of France, but was then called the Kingdom of the Franks.

Emperor Charlemagne, who valued education, wanted the people in his kingdom to learn to read and write. He himself could read a little, but never "got the hang" of writing. That was not unusual then, for in those days hardly anybody could write, let alone read. Charlemagne impressed upon his people the value of learning.

He collected books and had them copied in beautiful decorative script writing now known as Carolingian. His manuscripts were "illuminated," or as we would say, "illustrated," profusely. A few of these manuscripts still exist. Many people believe that our entire knowledge of classical literature is due to Charlemagne's efforts at copying all literature he could lay hold of.

Norsemen or Vikings

In the meantime, in addition to keeping the knowledge of Antiquity from getting lost forever, what else was going on in those Dark Ages? With the fall of Rome, tribes from the north strengthened their hold on what had been Roman territories all over Europe.

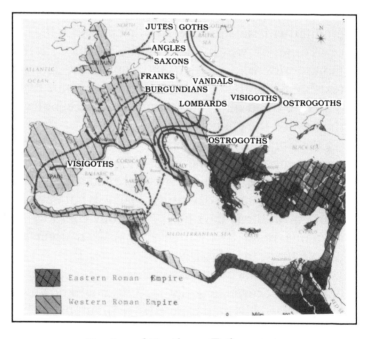

Routes of Northern Tribesmen

Small kingdoms developed where Roman rulers had once dominated. But there were vast areas without any form of government. In the early Medieval period each family had to find its own method of protection from the invading tribes, for the dreaded Vikings might at any time descend on a group of people, kill them, or take them away as slaves. Those who were not killed or kidnapped often had to "scrounge" for food, continually fearful of the Vikings.

Those who escaped death found life difficult. There was little reason to plant crops since fields were overrun by plundering tribesmen. And because of the onset of the bubonic plague, there was no sense of permanence or continuity into the future.

The Plague

The bubonic plague may have existed as a disease as early as the twelfth century B.C. It could have been the disease that struck the Philistines, referred to in the Old Testament as "Mice that mar the land." The epidemic which began in 541 A.D. around the Mediterranean, accounted for about 10,000 deaths in one day in Constantinople. Then it mysteriously disappeared for centuries, returning again near the end of the Medieval period in 1346. During the second epidemic the plague spread from ships landing at Marsailles, Genoa, and other seaports, where infected rats scurried ashore. By 1352 it is estimated that 25 million people had died all over Europe from the plague, or Black Death, as it was called because of the black body sores on its victims.

The plague is a disease caused by a bacillus transmitted by fleas to people. Fleas live on rodents such as rats, squirrels, chipmunks, etc., and when the infected rodents die, the fleas look for other host bodies, often humans, who, if untreated also die within about five days. Large pits were dug at the outskirts of towns, and wagons traveled through the towns each morning to pick up the dead for unceremonious burying.

During the outbreaks of the plague in the Medieval period, few people existed in the towns to carry on any businesses. Houses literally fell to the ground because there was no one to take care of them. There was only a scattering of people in the countryside to plow the fields or to bring in any crops. The plague and raids from the vikings contributed to the lack of economic growth during this period. It would not be until the plague had spent itself, and the vikings had been repeatedly repelled, that people in the Medieval period could begin to feel confident that there would be a future.

The Feudal System

As the saying goes, necessity is the mother of invention, and there was certainly a need for some kind of protective institution. Out of the chaos and this need for protection, the Medieval feudal system evolved.

A strong man who could build himself a fort or a castle would provide protection for other people, if, in turn, they would fight for him if he were attacked, or if he chose to attack another castle. In return, too,this strong man known as the Lord of the Manor, would provide the agricultural lands for his serfs, as they were called. The serfs raised crops for the Lords and Ladies of the castles. The Lord would provide a pittance of food to his serfs for their family use.

Many large stone castles were built for this feudal protective institution, which were often in the process of being enlarged, or repaired after a raid. Several of these castles exist today in western Europe.

Age of Chivalry

In the feudal system there were Lords and Ladies, knights and squires, serfs and troubadours and a style of manners known as chivalry. This system of manners represented in a small way the social system under which people agreed to live.

The laws of chivalry included certain niceties within the castles, and certain laws of honor outside the castle walls and on the battlefields. This was a time when one's word was one's honor, and honor was the thing that men fought and died for. From this Medieval period the customs and honor of knights such as King Arthur and his men are made legend.

Courtly Love

In this period, too, an interesting form of love between men and women developed, hitherto and henceforth unknown in history. Over the years, women had been treated in a variety of ways, either as slaves, or property, almost never with equality, and seldom as objects of romantic love, a style which evolved after the Medieval Period. This new kind of love was called Courtly Love because it developed in the courts of the Lords and Ladies of the feudal system. This strange kind of love flowered fresh and colorful into a world that needed some light-hearted gaiety.

It was taken for granted that practical reasons of merging lands dictated the reasons for marriage. As a consequence, if a man wanted love, he looked for it outside his own home. And the most desirable was the love one could sing of, to a high-born lady of a Lord's castle or court.

Often the lover or musician, and his lady love never actually spoke together. They knew of the adoration of the other, exchanged poetry through a messenger, but it was known as LOVE FROM AFAR. The more miserable the young male lover considered himself to be, the more "happy" was his state of life. Top culminate his love in any kind of physical contact would be to destroy his ecstasy. And for the lady's husband to get jealous would be a breach of etiquette. It was a matter of pride for a husband that his wife had a troubadour singing her praises. However, a husband's jealousy which did sometimes arise, was an occupational hazard of being a troubadour, the name given to the male courtly lovers.

The troubadours were long-haired musical composers. They awakened the people to a glimmer of joy through poetry and music and they gave a different importance to women. They launched a woman-centered poetry that dominated poetry for several hundreds of years. Unlike the poetry that came later, Troubadour Love Songs were addressed to another man's wife, something that the husband regarded as an honor. No one sang of love for his own wife, and unmarried women were not even considered as objects of love poetry.

Growth of Church Power

The troubadours were not of the masses, nor for the masses. For the peasants, life offered no such pleasure, or any pleasures that we know of. The serfs lived in fear, as they were virtually owned by their Lord. There was little more than work, poverty, and illness. A serf's life could be snuffed out by his Lord and his Lord had first claim on a serf's wife at any time. But even in despair there was some hope, kept alive through a growing belief in Christianity, which offered rewards, if not in this life, at least then in the After-Life in Heaven. Christianity told its believers that there was something better than the miserable life the serf lived on earth.

Gothic Cathedrals

The church, in its offer of hope, became a unifying force. The massive Gothic cathedrals which rose all over Europe in the Medieval Period, give testimony to the aspirations of the thousands of poor souls who labored at their stone construction in honor of God. The spires that reach to heaven could as well be the emaciated arms of the serfs lifted up in prayer. And, as the people turned to the church, the church grew rich and powerful.

Noblemen in their castles, and serfs on their feudal fiefs, the territory which the serfs worked, did not belong in a geographical country or even in a nation. But they did belong in an area governed religiously by the church. The church was the power of Europe in the Medieval period and it dominated the philosophy, the art, the architecture, and the music of the period.

The Crusades

The Crusades were another phenomenon of the Medieval Period -- a direct result of growing religious fervor. The Crusades began in 1097 for the purpose of recapturing Jerusalem from the infidels. Whoever the infidels happened to be depended on whether one is concerned with the First Crusade or the Fifth, or Sixth. On one crusade this could mean the Moslems, and on another crusade it could mean the Turks. In any event, the Crusades were mass pilgrimages to restore the Holy Land to the Christians.

The amazing thing about the Crusades is that the idea of all kinds of people, rich and poor, joined together thousands of souls in the eleventh century that in the seventh century were a disorganized, chaotic population with only one single idea and that was simply of being able to stay alive. Now, several hundred years later, under the banner of Christianity, the masses of people marched off with one driving purpose over thousands of miles and in tremendous hardship for the purpose of strengthening the birthplace of their religion. Christianity which grew slowly from its beginning, now, one thousands years later was the major power in the western world.

True, each Crusade, after wreaking considerable destruction in its path, became ineffective. With each Crusade, fewer people returned home. Many died on the way, many were taken captive and spent their lives in slavery in Egypt, many were killed in battles for the Holy Land. Starting a Crusade became a political thing for lords to do; religious motive gradually became secondary.

Probably the most disgraceful Crusade was the Children's Crusade in 1212. Thousands of children marched for weeks and months to reach the Holy Land, but ended up instead in the slave markets of Egypt. The growing disenchantment with "Crusading," meant that eventually they were abandoned entirely as a way of religious expression.

Growth of Trade

But what of the Crusades' effect? Did they accomplish what they set out to do? Sometimes they did. But if the Crusaders did wrest the Holy Land from the infidel, it was not for long. Something else happened as a result of the Crusades. While they had set out to squash the infidel, they actually succeeded in opening up trade between the Eastern world and the Western world and are in large part responsible for the beginning of the next historical period -- the Renaissance.

Prosperity depends on trade, and the trading and business houses in Florence, Italy, which was on the route from western Europe to the Holy Land, grew in wealth. Money was once again beginning to circulate in some quantity.

People could buy things which brought a sense of optimism. A new tradesman class grew in numbers and the goods from the Eastern world were carried farther up through Italy and then up into the northern part of Europe. The optimism spread.

End of the Dark Ages

Italy, where the Renaissance began, was the first country to come out of the moral and financial depression of the Medieval period. The tradesmen grew rich and as they wanted to possess nice things, they commissioned promising artists to do specific pieces of art. The church, too, which had become very rich with its large following and heavy taxation,

commissioned enormous works of art. A new feeling, a new idea, a new sense of possibilities would
grow stronger as the old feelings of despair made way
for a "Rebirth" of culture and learning. The "Light of
Learning" gleamed brighter and the Medieval
period, or Dark Ages, eventually came to an end.

THE RENAISSANCE

1400 - 1700

A period in history does not begin exactly in one year and end exactly in a certain year some centuries later. There is a carry-over of much of what went on in preceding years into the following period. Nor does an historical period begin at the same time in all areas. This is particularly true of the Renaissance which began in Florence, Italy, about 1440, but did not begin in Holland under different circumstances until much later.

However, Florence is the birthplace of the Renaissance, mainly because it was on the route to the Holy Land, through which many thousands of pilgrims passed during the Crusades. In the city of Florence the merchant class became powerful and their money influenced the styles in art, in fashion, and in architecture.

Rebirth of Learning

Before we get too far afield, it is important to know what exactly the Renaissance was and what its significance is to the study of humanity's search for the meaning of life. The word as we learned it means, "rebirth." But -- rebirth of what?

Essentially it was a rebirth of the desire to know about the knowledge that had at one time been known -- knowledge that had been lost after the collapse of Rome and barely kept alive by the monks in their monasteries, and by the efforts of men like Charlemagne. Initially the Renaissance was a looking back to Antiquity.

There was a resurgence of interest in the literature of the epic poems of Homer and Virgil and in the philosophy of the Greeks. Socrates, Plato, and Aristotle were the first teachers of the intellectual Renaissance men. People were coming out of their financial and moral depression and exploring their creativity. Aristotle's logic and his scientific theories provided a good frame work for the scientific starting points of this new period.

More people could read, and with the invention of the printing press there was more to read. The *Bible* was printed in the language of each country instead of in Latin only, and for the first time people could interpret the Bible for themselves. This was dangerous for the power of the church and in no small part led to the Reformation and eventually to Protestantism.

The Rise of Nationalism and Monarchies

The political power of the Medieval period -- the church -- gave way to a new power -- money. With money came the rise of nations. Lords of castles could pay men to fight in their armies and they could establish themselves as kings over larger and larger territories. But, no matter how else the Western world seemed to be going, its people wanted art forms. The very wealthy patrons and several Popes commissioned great artists to create the master-pieces that have been inspiration to humanity ever since. The ceiling of the Sistine Chapel is one of the many examples of this kind of creative "arrange-ment" between sponsor and artist.

Rethinking Science

Tied into this new feeling of confidence were the new thrusts made in the field of science. In reviewing the old concepts of man's place in the universe, especially the theories of Aristotle and Ptolemy that the universe revolved around the earth, the Renaissance scientists saw the flaws in the an-cient theories. They used the philosophical techni-ques of Aristotle's logic, which became part of the scientific method, and with scientific instruments they reversed the earth's place in the universe.

Copernicus proved, through the scientific method, that the earth revolved around the sun, and Galileo, with the newly invented telescope, strengthened Copernicus' theory. Galileo also added the knowledge about the force of gravity.

New scientific inventions expanded what was known about the unknown. The microscope, in-vented about 1590, revealed the world of micro-or-ganisms. This meant that the old theory that life spontaneously created itself was no longer valid. The microscope helped in identifying and controlling in-fectious diseases and proved that specific infections are caused by specific microbes. At this time the thermometer was also invented and it had many uses, both in public health and in industry. Galileo used the telescope, invented in 1608, to strengthen Copernicus' theory about the earth revolving around the sun. That produced great controversy in the Church which, at that time, maintained, in spite of scientific evidence, that the earth was the center of the universe.

Galileo introduced the idea of gravity. The year that Galileo died, Newton was born. He is said to be one of the greatest scientific minds that the world has known. He expanded on Galileo's laws of gravity and added his own laws of motion.

Classical Architecture

Architecturally, Renaissance builders looked back to the Greek and Roman ruins and reconstructed the classical lines in the buildings of the Renaissance. In the late Renaissance, an art form of its own period developed which was seen in the exterior and interior building decoration. This was known as BAROQUE (1600-1750) and replaced the somber straight lines of classicism with circles and ornate decorations. The highly decorative Baroque style was carried over into music.

Complex Music

The simple melodies and chants of the Medieval period lasted through much of the Renaissance, but toward the end, about 1600, with the in-

vention of new instruments, and with the more live-
ly spirit abounding at the time, music became complex and involved. It became an important art form
in its own right. In 1685 Johann Sebastian Bach was
born, to become one of the great composers we still
enjoy today. He was only the first of many who soon
brought a new and very serious dimension to music
as an art to be enjoyed and studied. This will be discussed further in the history of music section.

Global Exploration

While the Crusaders had opened up trade
routes through Italy, others were opening up trade
routes around the world at this time. Inventions such
as the sextant, which was an improvement of the
mariner's astralobe, made it possible for sea
voyagers to chart their course with better accuracy.
During these early Renaissance years Amerigo
Vespucci sailed probably to Cape Canaveral,
Florida, believing he had landed in Asia a year
before Columbus came to America.Vasco da Gama
commanded the fleet which first completed the trip
to India going around the Cape of Good Hope,
thereby establishing a trade route between Europe
and the Orient.

Christopher Columbus, in attempting to establish a trade route to the Orient, instead landed in
America. Ferdinand Magellan was the first man to
sail around the world, though in fact, he was killed
by natives on an island he was trying to capture
before the voyage was completed. His ships sailed

on, however, establishing Magellan as a foremost explorer. The Straits of Magellan, at the tip of South America, are named after him. It took him five weeks to navigate his ships through these turbulent waters. All of these explorations opened up new vistas for further expansion, and trade and communication for people in the Renaissance.

Creative Confidence

Whenever a country is in a financial depression, as it was for about a thousand years, there is a depression of human creative spirit which seems to say, "What's the use?" But as people begin to experience a slightly better mode of life, and new possibilities are envisioned, they see that there may be hope after all. Renaissance artists found their efforts rewarded. There was money to pay for works of art, and art itself became one of the mediums through which people found confidence in themselves which had been lost for so long.

It seemed that the floodgates were opened and creativity in every field flowed forth. Poets explored the epic poetry of Homer and Virgil of Antiquity, they read and enjoyed the Troubadour Love Songs and poems of Courtly Love, and then went on to write their own. Global exploration opened up new vistas, and new possibilities in other lands. The Renaissance was an era of confidence which comes with success.

MODERN PERIOD

1700 - THE PRESENT

We are so accustomed to at least giving "lip service" to the equality of human beings that it is difficult to put ourselves in other civilizations and times when this was not a serious philosophical concept. But at no historical time before the modern period (except possibly Prehistoric) was the life of the common or lower class people of much importance to society.

From Antiquity on, whether it was Priest, or shaman, emperor, feudal lord, or king, the rulers wielded life and death power over the common people. The average person depended on a ruler's mercy, not on his or her own rights, which were almost non-existent. One was either a slave or a non-voting freedman, or a woman whose husband, if he didn't have actual life and death power over his wife, had the right to beat her.

When the territories held by the feudal lords in the Medieval period were unified into nations, the rulers assumed the Divine Right of Kings, an idea that had come from the Egyptian Pharaohs. The Pharaohs, you remember, were considered gods. The Kings in these later years did just as the Ancient Pharaohs did in exercising their Divine Right over their subjects. Today the practice of Presidents or Governors granting clemency or pardons to convicted criminals comes from the philosophy of the Divine Right of Kings.

When Europe was unifying into nations, a growing class of moneyed people -- the merchants -- who had come into prominence in the Renaissance, were gaining and exercising power over the people who toiled for the merchants. This merchant class developed a new era -- the most significant change in the way people lived since the Age of Cultivation began about 15,000 B.C.

Industrial Revolution

As more goods were desired, people moved into towns to work in factories which developed as the Industrial Revolution gathered force. In the factories and coal mines, appalling labor conditions and exploitation of the poor were the rule rather than the exception. It was common practice in England, for instance, for children as young as eight years old to work 16 hours a day, deep in the coal mines, pulling trolleys that weighed many times their own weight, seven days a week, never seeing the light of day. These and other conditions of the poor prompted Charles Dickens to write his social novels.

An actual report of a labor reformer named Michael Sadler, investigating the working conditions of children in the mills of England, is available to us, known as the Sadler Report, from the Committee on the Bill to Regulate the Labour of Children in the Mills and Factories of the United Kingdom (London: The House of Commons, 1832):

Michael Thomas Sadler, Esquire, in the Chair calls in Matthew Crabtree. - - At what age did you first go to work in the blanket mill? - - Eight. - - Will you state the hours of labour... - - From 6 in the morning until 8 at night. - - Fourteen hours? - - Yes. - - With what intervals for refreshment and rest? - - An hour at noon. - - Were you always on time? - - No. - - What was the consequence if you had been late? - - I was most commonly beaten. - - What was your situation in the mill? - - I was a piecener. - - Will you state to this Committee whether piecening is a very laborious employment for children, or not? - - It is a very laborious employment. Pieceners are continually running to and fro, and on their feet the whole day. - - The duty of the piecener is to take the cardings from one part of the machinery, and to place them on another? - - Yes. - - State the conditions of the children toward the latter part of the day, who have thus to keep up with the machinery. - - It is as much as they can do when they are not very much fatigued to keep up with their work, and toward the close of the day, when they come to be more fatigued, they cannot keep up with it very well, and the consequence is that they are beaten to spur them on. - - And is it your belief that if you and the other children had not been so beaten, you should not have got through the work? - - I should not if I had not been kept to it by some means. - - What is the effect of this piecening upon the hands? - - It makes them bleed; the skin is completely rubbed off, and in that case they bleed in perhaps a dozen parts... The hands can never be hardened in that work, for the grease keeps them soft and continual rubbing is always wearing them down. - - Were there girls as well as boys employed and if so were they more tenderly treated by the overlookers, or were they worked and beaten in the same manner? - - There were girls and there was no difference in their treatment. - - You seem to say that this beating is absolutely necessary, in order to keep the children up to their work; is it universal throughout all factories? - - I have been in several other factories, and I have witnessed the same cruelty in them all.

Eventually child labor laws were passed limiting the number of hours a child was permitted to work in coal mines or factories. At first, these new laws permitted employers to work children ten hours a day. This was gradually reduced.

Age of Enlightenment and Age of Reason

These are the names given to two periods when writers, philosophers and scientists attempted to establish by reason what one should believe. Roughly, The Age of Reason was in the 17th century and The Age of Enlightenment was in the 18th century. The Age of Reason produced profound changes in what people thought. It was a period of philosophical revolution. But the thinking was limited to a few elite intellectuals like Locke, Descartes and Pascal. Pascal has been described as one of the most comprehensive geniuses the world has know.

The main emphasis in the new way of thinking was that people should be autonomous, that is, they should govern themselves. All people are capable of reasoning and should use this capability to govern themselves.

John Locke, (1632 - 1704), an Englishman wrote, "Our reason teaches us that mankind ...being all equal and independent, no one ought to harm another in his life, health, liberty, or possession." He also said that government should be a compact of mutual consent to provide the greatest good for the greatest number, adding that people GIVE to their government the power for that government to govern the people. And if the government goes beyond the power given to it, the people have not only the right to revolt, but a duty to create revolution in order to preserve their government.

The concerns of the Age of Reason were for the common people. People should chose their governmental leaders and tell them what they want done. Dignity should not be reserved just for the powerful. All people should have the right to speak freely. These ideas were unheard of by the general population before The Age of Reason.

But it took the philosophers in the next century, in The Age of Enlightenment, to publicize the ideas of The Age of Reason. One of the most famous of these philosophers is Voltaire who said the aim of life should be the pursuit of human happiness, to make better the human condition0on. He tried to break the mold of how people had thought, to get them to use their own reason rather than the view s of those in authority.

Other Enlightenment philosophers were Hume, Paine, Rousseau, Diderot and Montesquieu. Rousseau added his own ideas to those of Locke, and added that government by one man is tyranny. As can be imagined, these ideas challenged the Divine Right of Kings and helped to bring on the French Revolution which toppled France's King Louis IVX.

It is interesting to note how many heretofore unthinkable ideas came out of this early modern period known as the Age of Enlightenment, such as:

1. The Equality of Man
2. The right to choose one's government.
3 The duty to revolt if the elected rulers usurp (go beyond) the power given to them by the electorate.
4. The rise of democracies.

The enlightened thinking and writing became popular reading material. It gathered followers, activists and led to the downfall of many monarchies and to the rise of democracies such as France, England, and the United States.

It was a difficult period of transition for the Western World. The change from the power of kings to the power of the people was bloody. In the late 1770's the American Revolution and the French

Revolution gave power to the people via a military revolution. Since that time the common or middle class and even lower class people have been assuming rights and exercising power throughout the Western World.

The Struggle for Equality

Breaking the bonds of the injustice of unequal rights has been the common person's struggle during the whole of the modern period, and is still a strong social force today. What, for instance, are the groups that feel the injustice of their treatment in today's society? Foremost in our minds might be the Blacks and other racial groups. More recently women have been seeking their own justice. There is a much longer history of prejudice against women than against Blacks. This inequality of treatment goes back to myths and in reality to the beginning of history.

Any group's efforts to "right" what they consider to be the "wrongs" of being treated unequally are their revolutions. Currently there are revolutions in most of the established social institutions, such as the institution of marriage, the institution of education, and the institution of religion. But any institution which is going to survive must change with the times.

Summary

As we begin the twenty-first century, we can look back over 5000 years of civilization. We can see what people have accomplished and we can read what they have thought. We can ponder the same philosophical questions that have plagued human beings since civilization began. We also ask ourselves some new and profound questions which the modern period has provoked.

What are these age-old questions and how have they been answered through the historical periods? What are the new questions, and what answers can we give? This is the time to turn to a short history of philosophy, to examine the purpose of philosophy and a small part of its body of knowledge.

CHAPTER TWO

PHILOSOPHY

Introduction

The word "philosophy" sounds profound and maybe even formidable enough to make one want to turn away from it. Yet we are involved in philosophy continuously one way or another. Every decision we make is based on our own philosophy. First, there is the decision which we all face each morning of whether or not to get out of bed. Then, when we do get up, we make decisions determined by our philosophy of life.

You may not be aware that you are consciously set on a course of action determined by your philosophy. The very fact that you are reading this page tells you something about your philosophy of life. You may be saying that you are reading this page because you have to, or, because there is nothing else to do. But nobody physically forced you to sit in the chair you occupy and nobody forced you to read this. You could choose not to. In fact, there are almost always other choices, including the choice of doing nothing.

You are reading this because there is some pleasure in it, or some future reward that makes the reading worth the effort. The action now, or the reward you seek later, is determined by what philosophical concepts you value. If you say you don't have a choice, you are simply denying the responsibility for your own thinking related to what you consciously or unconsciously feel as the meaning of your life. And that is what philosophy is all about: A SEARCH FOR THE MEANING OF LIFE.

Each historical period evokes its own questions about its times. In trying to answer these questions, we are searching for the meaning of life of the times. In this modern period, the threat of a nuclear explosion and the exploitation of the earth's resources, either combined or separately, can cause the end of human life. These threats give us pause now and then to re-evaluate our day-to-day existence. Periodic insecurities and disenchantment with "the system" give rise to social groups who have been labeled, "Bohemians," "Beatniks," "Hippies," "Punks."

The Vietnam War, the Watergate and Iran-Contra scandals, the age of computers, the increased terrorism, the drug craze, have all affected our thinking and provoked questions that direct us in our search for meaning.

What, for instance, was the meaning of the Vietnam war? How do the Watergate and Iran-Contra scandals affect our thinking about government and justice? Are people becoming insignificant in a computer and robot age? What are the methods of protecting one's property and one's life in the wake of a surge of terrorism and in a drug culture? Who has the "rights" in these cases? How do all these things and more cause us to re-evaluate our purpose and the meaning of our own individual lives? Whether it is drugs, or the stock-piling of nuclear armaments, any significant change in a particular historical period affects and often changes definitions of the meaning of life for that time.

Let's look at some important changes and discoveries which caused people to change the way they related to their place in the universe. We are each of us a part of our total environment. We do not exist in our own individual vacuum. When men landed on the moon, that changed our perspective of our environment and of our place in the total universal scheme.

Think carefully about each of the following that happened in history and determine what difference each of these made on the way the individual might have felt about her or his place in their world:

1. Until about 1500 A.D. people believed that the earth was the center of the universe. Both Aristotle and Ptolemy had put forth the theory and supported it with the scientific evidence of

their day. Around 1500, Copernicus taught that the sun was the center of the universe.

2. In the same historical period as the above, Galileo discovered the telescope.

3. Also, in the same period, Columbus discovered America.

4. In the modern period we have invented nuclear bombs, which give human beings the potential to annihilate themselves.

5. In the modern period we have landed on the moon, can send astronauts into space and bring them back again in the same space ship.

6. Manual work has been automated to the extent that machines,computers, and robots gain importance over human labor.

7. The development of the contraceptive pill has given relatively safe and inexpensive population control to the world.

What are the philosophical questions that each of the above presented to the world at the time?

Needless to say, these are only a few examples of the many changes that have caused people to reconsider their place, purpose, and ultimately the meaning of human life. Change is the nature of life and there have always been people who reflect more profoundly on life than other people do. Or at least there are some who make their reflections known one way or another to the rest of the world. You will become acquainted with a few major philosophers here whose thinking has come down to us through the ages:

Zoroaster . . about 1000 BC
Socrates . . 469 BC - 399 BC
Plato . . . . . 427 BC - 347 BC
Aristotle . 384 BC - 322 BC
Aquinas . . . 1227 AD - 1274
Locke . . . . . 1632 AD - 1704
Nietzsche . 1844 AD - 1900

Depending on one's point of view, these men may or may not be considered the greatest philosophers. (Religion, which will be discussed in the next section, is philosophy too. The difference between religion and philosophy relies on the shade of meaning between establishing an idea by reasoning and establishing an idea by faith.) Most philosophers respond either negatively or positively toward religion.

The philosophers selected for this study represent a certain philosophy for their period in history, though other people compiling another list would undoubtedly choose other men for other reasons.

The study of each philosopher will begin with a short discussion of his family background, if it is known. Then there will be a short resume of the philosopher's main ideas, followed by a short excerpt of his writing, if any has come down to us. In this way you can see for yourself the style and the content.

You may notice that the questions these men have attempted to answer in their time in history are questions that we have asked ourselves in our own time. Historically, people search for their purpose in life, and in the search they bump up against the same questions and similar answers throughout history. Here are some questions which perplex people periodically. How would you answer them for yourself?

1. Who am I?
2. Why am I alive?
3. What is my relationship to the universe?
4. What is permanent and what is changeable?
5. Do I have an obligation to my fellow human being?
6. How can a person find the truth?
7. Is there a God?
8. Does justice exist? If not, why not? If so, why?

ZOROASTER

About 1000 B.C.

Persia

Persia, which is now Iraq and Iran, was the birth place of Zoroaster, the "Father of Philosophy." There are many mythical stories as to his origin, and some say he had a divine conception. No one really knows of his beginnings or his life. His birth date is said to be anywhere from 1000 BC to 600 BC.

The Persians called him Zarathustra, but the Greeks, who took much of their knowledge from Persia, re-named him Zoroaster which was his original birth name -- Zarathustra Spitama -- a name which indicates he was born into a warrior clan. Plato, Pliny, and Plutarch wrote of Zoroaster, though some of their writings are legendary. Literature, however, tells us that he had three wives and six children.

His philosophy, Zoroastrianism, was at one time a religion practiced all through the Eastern world. It is still practiced today in Bombay, India, by the Parsees, and in a few scattered places throughout the world. Though Zoroastrianism began as a religion, we study it now as a philosophy because the concepts which have endured are based more on ethical conduct than on spiritual ideas.

All philosophers reflect the ideas that were of concern to the people during their period in history. At the time of Zoroaster, conditions in Persia were incredibly harsh. Human torture was a common happening.

There is the legend of the farmer who had lost all his sons except one in battles. He appealed to the ruler to spare his last young son and not conscript him for war. The ruler had the son cut in two pieces and his columns of soldiers marched over the son's remains so that the other fathers could see.

Another story tells of a woman being skinned alive when she asked for mercy for stealing. But where, Zoroaster asked, could one find mercy? Why did the gods allow such suffering? Or, if there were gods, what good were they if most of the people were required to suffer? Why did the gods allow all the evil in the world?

In trying to search out the answers to his questions and ultimately determine the meaning of human life in those cruel times, Zoroaster concluded that a person is a sort of battleground wherein good and evil struggle for power. People, he said, have the choice of doing good or evil. It is a matter of choosing the right action. This theme is repeated throughout history by people who ponder the necessity for evil and suffering.

But what then, one would have asked of Zoroaster, of evil that happens to people, evil over which they have no control. How does Zoroaster explain this? This question and the same answer are repeated by other philosophers born hundreds of years later.

Zoroaster explained that evil is the necessary contrast that demonstrates the value of good. If one never knew evil, one would never know how good is. This idea comes from 1000 B.C., but only in the last few years it was repeated by a modern philosopher, George Bernard Shaw, who said that a constant holiday is a definition of a living Hell. But people, Zoroastrianism preaches, have the ability to choose good or evil. And if one chooses evil, there is no retribution, no atonement, no one to intercede for the sinner, no offerings to erase the action. One will be held responsible for her or his actions in the afterlife, descending to a horrible hell or ascending to paradise.

The purpose of suffering, Zoroaster preached, is to know by contrast when things are good. How can we enjoy rest, if we don't know work? Zoroaster said that all life is a struggle of good over evil. One can see God in the good that people do, he claimed. Otherwise why would people do good things? He said that God is working through people on earth.

Zoroaster's God was Ahura-Mazda, the Lord of Light. It was difficult for him to convert people to a One-God philosophy at a time when many gods were worshipped in the communities. Ahura Mazda, was the same god the people had been worshipping, but Zoroaster claimed that this god was the *only* god. All others gods were false gods.

His book was the *Avesta*, wherein he outlined the moral conduct for fighting evil and doing good. Except for a few followers today, Zoroastrianism was eliminated by the Moslems by 650 A.D., though we still look to his thinking as the beginnings of philosophy. He is considered the father of philosophy.

SOCRATES

469-399 B.C.

Greece

We'll take a look now at the philosophies of men who have left their historical mark more clearly than Zoroaster. We know something about Socrates, the way he lived, and what his family was like, his mother a midwife, and his father a stonemason. He was not a very good provider for his wife and children. He did some sculpturing, but he wasn't very good at it and he made little money.

He was much more interested in cultivating the mind of young men than in making a living. We have reference to him as being rather homely, with a large bulbous nose and a stocky figure. He was vigorous, capable of enduring physical hardship and he could drink most men "under the table."

Unlike Zoroaster's philosophy which comes to history by word of mouth, Socrates' philosophy was written almost entirely by his most famous pupil, Plato.

Socrates' philosophy was not as much in the area of ideas, as it was in the area of technique -- the technique of helping people find the truth for themselves. Socrates was a questioner. Relentlessly he probed and questioned people, not to satisfy a curiosity of his own, but to get people to hear their own answers and to examine their thinking and ultimately arrive at the truth. His famous quote is, "The unexamined life is not worth living." He upturned old opinions to get people to examine their purposes and ideas.

Young men gathered around Socrates. He asked them questions about justice and honesty and courage and other values. Being a great respecter of government, he concentrated his questioning on man's relationship to his government. He wanted his students to recognize the ingredients of justice and the individual citizen's responsibility for justice.

When his students answered his questions he would question their answers. Then they would answer again, and he would question those answers. The process of a teacher's asking questions that help the student search out answers became known as the SOCRATIC METHOD OF TEACHING. This type of teaching is favorably contrasted with the method that simply requires a student to memorize what the teacher puts before the student. Socrates refers to his kind of teaching as a type of midwifery. explaining that he helped students give birth to knowledge which they could formulate for themselves when he asked the incisive questions which brought forth truth. He said that the difference from what a regular midwife did and what he did was that he attended men and not women and that he helped men give birth to their ideas. He claimed that the pangs of giving birth to ideas and truths were worse than the labor pains of women in childbirth. He also said that he never taught anybody anything, that he only helped them deliver their own thoughts clearly.

In Plato's Dialogues, "*I Am a Philosophical Midwife*," Socrates is speaking to Theaetetus when he says,

> My art of midwifery is in most respects like theirs; but differs, in that I attend men and not women and I look after their souls where they are in labor, and not after their bodies; and the triumph of my art is in thoroughly examining whether the thought which the mind of the young man brings forth is a false idol or a noble and true birth. And like the midwives I am barren, and the reproach which is often made against me that I ask questions of others and have not the wit to answer them myself, is very just -- the reason is, that the god compels me to be a midwife but does not allow me to bring forth. And therefore I am not myself at all wise, nor have I anything to show which is the invention of birth of my own soul, but those who converse with me profit. Some of them appear dull enough at first, but afterwards, as our acquaintance ripens, if the god is gracious to them, they all make astonishing progress; and this is in the opinion of others as well as in their own.

Socrates prompted young people to think in order to learn. Instead of learning by rote memory, they were learning to search out their own truths. This probing was a disturbance and it caused problems in the city of Athens. The city fathers became annoyed because they wanted their young men to accept the knowledge as it was given to them, not to be searching into deeper meanings nor questioning their own fathers. The problem between Socrates and the city fathers became so difficult that one of the fathers of a pupil of Socrates encouraged the city government of Athens to bring Socrates to trial. Socrates was a threat to the establishment and as such he was charged with corrupting the youth. A sign was posted on the walls of the public building. Socrates is guilty of a double crime: first, for not worshiping the gods whom the city worships: next, for corrupting the youth. The penalty for this crime is death.

His jury? Five hundred uneducated farmers and tradesmen. He was condemned to death.

Those who knew Socrates and loved him deeply believed that the death verdict was unjust. He had committed no evil, they said, he had simply helped people to learn to think. His friends were grieved and they made arrangements for his escape from prison. His pupil, Plato, helped arrange the escape. There were plans made for him to live out his life in safety and in exile, but Socrates refused to escape. It is as important to know about the death of Socrates as it is to know of his life, for his death epitomized one very important aspect of his philosophy.

His answer to those who would help him was that he had expected the law to protect him when he had needed it and therefore he must obey the law, even if he believed that in this case it was unjust, or else he would be destroying government. His death is a lesson in his philosophy: he taught by example.

What we know of Socrates we read from Plato, who fled the city of Athens after Socrates' death, returning years later to set up his Academy of Learning.

On the day that Socrates was to drink the hemlock, his concern was for his friends. He did not want them to grieve. He asked what the symptoms of the poison would be and when he felt the effects of it, he lay down, bidding his friends good-bye and asking that an offering be made to the god of healing.

PLATO

427-347 B.C.

Greece

Socrates was a poor man and homely. By contrast, his most famous pupil, Plato, was a rich young man and handsome. Plato was shocked and saddened by the verdict of the death penalty for his teacher. He absented himself from Athens for many years, but returned at the age of forty to set up the Academy of Learning. He believed that if the citizens of the jury had been educated, that the verdict for Socrates would have been different. Education of the citizens became a prime goal for Plato.

Like Socrates, Plato believed that truth began with two. He taught that discussions and questions were necessary for arriving at the truth, and that a person alone could not find the truth. Both men believed that truth is not given, but that each person must search it out with great effort. His writings are in the form of conversations with two or more people discussing -- in other words -- in dialogue.

Plato wrote thirty of these *Dialogues* in which he examines questions that perplexed the people of Antiquity. He put Socrates' words, along with his ideas, into conversational writing. His ideas on education were proposed in his dialogue, *The*

Republic. Education in Plato's ideal state, as he presented his ideas, would be like this:

When children were ten years old they would be taken from their parents to spend the next ten years in strengthening their bodies and learning music. Harmony was important to Plato, but to him it meant the inclusive harmony of mathematics, religion, and history.

For the next ten years, from ages twenty to thirty, students would learn science. Those who failed would be relegated to lowest class of citizens.

When people reached the age of thirty, if they failed the tests they would become middle class citizens. Those who passed the tests would have the potential to become future rulers. The last five years would be devoted to the study of philosophy in order to acquaint students with the world of ideas in contrast to the world of things.

As you can see, only the most highly educated would be prepared for leadership to rule. To be a ruler one would need to know and understand Plato's *Philosophy of Ideas* which has been discussed and redefined through the past two thousand years. It is almost impossible to explain clearly, especially in a short space. On the other hand, it is not the purpose of this work to go deeply into each subject, but rather to give the reader some acquaintance with the many fields of creative development.

As to this *Philosophy of Ideas*, Plato wrote that everything exists in the mind of God and anything that is outside the mind of God is merely an example of the perfect, or ideal thing or thought which is in the mind of God. (Since the concept of a one-

God was not at that time accepted in Greece, it is not clear which god Plato means, or if God is referring to a supernatural power undefined.) Nevertheless, in his philosophy he said that everything and every idea is a reflection and that reality exists only in the mind of God. People who see things as things are prisoners and are not fit to rule. Only those who can see IDEAS are qualified to rule because they have survived such temptations as greed, hate, ambition, and jealousy. Once they have survived those impulses, they are fit to rule because they can see that ideas are more important than things, especially the idea of justice.

You can understand that Plato would be vitally concerned with education after having seen his teacher, Socrates, brought to death by the verdict of an uneducated mob. You can also understand his concern for justice which he equated with harmony, saying that if there is harmony in the state, that would prove there is justice. "Justice is to the soul, what health is to the body."

If you have ever been treated unfairly, you know the turmoil and frustration you experienced. It is not a peaceful, harmonious condition. Your mind and body are in disequilibrium. If, in your family life there is harmony, Plato would say that should prove that there is justice in your home. If there is harmony between you and your teacher or employer, or personal relationships, that would prove there is justice and that you are being treated fairly.

Each of Plato's dialogues explores a different subject. In "*Meno*," for instance, he asks, "Can virtue be taught?" Or for that matter, can anything be taught? Plato is writing about a dialogue between Socrates and Menon, a Greek nobleman.

> SOCRATES: There now, let us take virtue ...If virtue is a quality among the things which are about the soul, would virtue be teachable, or not? First, if it is like or unlike knowledge, can it be taught or not, or as we said just now, can it be remembered...Or is it plain to everyone that only one thing is taught to men, and that is knowledge? MENON: So it seems to me at least. S: Then if virtue is a knowledge, it is plain that it could be taught. M: Of course... S: Now we have to consider, as it seems, whether virtue is a knowledge or something distinct from knowledge...Don't we say that virtue is a good thing? This hypothesis holds for us, that it is good? M: We do say so. S: Then if there is something good, and yet separate from knowledge, possibly virtue would not be a knowledge, but if there is no good which knowledge does not contain, it would be a right notion to suspect that it is a knowledge...It can be taught if it is knowledge...But I have my doubts whether it is knowledge...If a thing can be taught--anything, not virtue only--must there not be both teachers and learners of it? M: Yes, I think so. S: On the contrary, again, if there are neither teachers nor learners, we might fairly assume the thing cannot be taught? M: That is true; but don't you think there are teachers of virtue?

There is then a discussion of men who have taught their sons to be great horsemen, good in the fine arts, and in gymnastics, but who were not taught virtue, though, as Socrates says, the fathers had great power and money and could have had their sons taught in virtue as well as in other things. But, he says, as there are no teachers of virtue, there are no learners. The following are excerpts from a lengthy discourse.

S: Well, it seemed that it could be taught if virtue was wisdom. M: Yes. S: And if it could be taught, it would be wisdom. M: Certainly. S: And if there were teachers, it could be taught, if no teachers, it could not? M: Just so. S: Further, we agreed that there were no teachers of it? M: That is true. S: We agreed then, that it could not be taught, and that it was not wisdom? M: Certainly. S: But, however, we agree that it is good? M: Yes. S: And that which guides rightly is useful and good? M: Certainly. S: Again, only these two things guide rightly, right opinion and knowledge; and if a man has these, he guides rightly -- for things which happen rightly from some chance do not come about by human guidance: but in all things in which a man is a guide towards which is right, these two do it, true opinion and knowledge. M: I think so. S: Well, since it cannot be taught, no longer is virtue knowledge. M: I think not. S: Then it was not by wisdom, or because they were wise, that such men guided the cities...they could not make others like themselves, because not knowledge made them what they were. M: Excellently said, I think, Socrates. S: Then from this our reasoning, Menon, virtue is shown as coming to us, whenever it comes, by divine dispensing....

ARISTOTLE

384-322 B.C.

Greece

Aristotle is the third of the three most famous Greek philosophers. He came as a student to Plato's Academy of Learning and was not at first well received by Plato, who considered Aristotle to be a young man more interested in his appearance and fancy clothes than in learning. Plato came to recognize, though, that the brightest mind in the Academy was Aristotle's. He had a keen interest in many subjects, including a curiosity about science which he developed from his father's medical practice.

When Plato died, Aristotle left Athens and became a tutor to the son of King Philip of Macedonia. This son later became Alexander the Great. The household of King Philip was violent, arbitrary, and tempestuous. Aristotle saw the courtly bickering, and the cruel and instantaneous injustice of King Philip. The king and queen fought ferociously both verbally and physically and the king and his young son, Alexander, flew into many fights, nearly killing each other with whatever weapon they could find at the moment.

From all of the violence that he saw, Aristotle came to believe that people needed to be tamed and

that taming the heart was a primary object of education. He saw his young prince, Alexander, give way
to his violent temper at any whim. From this, Aristotle learned to hold himself in check. He said that
holding oneself in check is the best protection
against violence in the world. He believed that because men can wield murderous weapons, they are
the deadliest of all animals.

When Philip's queen hired a man to assas-
sinate her husband, Alexander dismissed Aristotle
and set out to conquer the world. One of the first
things that the young Alexander did was put
Aristotle's nephew to death for not worshiping the
new king as a god. Aristotle decided it was time to
leave Macedonia.

There was then said to be two strong forces
in the world: the intelligent, calming influence of
Aristotle who was determined to teach, and the fero-
cious influence of Alexander the Great, who was
determined to conquer the world. Alexander was a
strange mixture of passion and compassion. One
story tells of a young dancing girl who complained
that she did not have any light to see her way home.
Alexander is said to have set fire to the palace of the
King of Persia, saying that should give her light
enough.

Aristotle reacted to all his violence by
developing his philosophy of the Golden Mean.
Human error, he said, is expressed in terms of too
much, too soon, too little. The wise man chooses a
course midway between two extremes. For instance,
when we are faced with danger, which way shall we
act, as a coward or as a heedless dare-devil? Or when

we are striving for bodily health, shall we go for days without eating, or eat excessively? It sounds only reasonable to choose a sensible course, but Aristotle believed that happiness depended on each person's choosing the Golden Mean and on knowing what choice of action was best for themselves. By that he did not mean the choice that would please a parent, or a teacher, or a friend, but the choice that fitted the individual. Unhappiness, he said, was the result of poor choice of action. Also, he would add, a happy person is a gentle person.

His scientific interest led to his development of a Zoological Garden and a Museum of Natural History. He carried this scientific thinking into a system of reasoning which we call logic. He termed his system "syllogisms," a scientific procedure in thinking which should lead to correct conclusions.

A syllogism is a set of these three statements:

1. General premise
2. Specific premise
3. Conclusion

Example:
1. General premise - Albert belongs to a class of animals.
2. Specific premise - Albert is rational (he thinks)
3. Conclusion - Albert is rational animal.

Remember, during the Renaissance people looked back to the thinkers of Antiquity for knowledge. Renaissance scientists picked up on

Aristotle's scientific, logical thinking and applied the process to the scientific explorations into the law of gravity, the composition of the universe, the properties of force, and innumerable other ideas which need proof or rejection, based on evidence and logical conclusions.

In syllogisms, as you can see there are three chances for error. If there is a mistake in the general premise, the beginning assumption is incorrect and the conclusion will be wrong. If in the specific premise the subject is not of the same class as is referred to in the general premise, the conclusion will be wrong. And the final chance for error is in the area of the subject if it might not be in the same class as in the specific premise.

In any correct syllogisms one can apply this pattern:
General premise - A is B
Specific premise - C is A
Conclusion - C is B

Here are some examples of incorrect syllogisms:
General premise - All insects are good swimmers.
Specific premise - A bee is an insect.
Conclusion - Bees are good swimmers.

Apply the above pattern to determine where it became invalid.
General premise - All birds have feathers.
Specific premise - A sparrow is a bird.
Conclusion - Therefore, Lassie has feathers.

Where in the above example did the syllogism become invalid?

Aristotle pointed out also that correct thinking could not be obtained if one used fallacies (false statements from which one proceeded) or ambiguities (words with more than one meaning.)

The science of logical thinking began with Aristotle and has been with us for 2000 years. Some of his actual scientific theories were destroyed under closer examination with the invention of the telescope and when the law of gravity was determined. Nevertheless, Aristotle is still considered to be one of the greatest intellects in history. And most of the philosophers since his time are considered to be either Platonists (those who ascribe to Plato's ideas), or Aristotelians.

The two men differed in their field of emphasis. Plato was concerned with statesmanship and Aristotle with science. Aristotle had some strong concerns for government, but they did not occupy his thinking as much as his interest in science. Governmentally he was interested in every citizen having an adequate amount of money to live on. A seething mob of discontented citizens, he said, is a threat to a government.

Both men emphasized the need for educating citizens, Plato because he affirmed that the most intelligent should rule, and Aristotle because he believed that intelligent action and restraint would eliminate violence.

Socrates, Plato, and Aristotle all differed in their views on religion. Socrates did not have much interest in the gods. He believed more in the mind of the people. Plato, however, was quite religious, believing in the after-life and philosophizing that "now" was just an interlude. Aristotle, like Socrates, said that the nearest thing to God was intellectual questioning and that everything reaches its full potential in this life.

These three Greek philosophers were part of the Golden Age of Greece that lasted for about 500 years. When this Golden Age came to an end, the Roman Empire was spreading its culture around the European continent, but it took with it part of the Greek culture. For the Romans had brought Greek tutors into their homes to teach their children who were consequently reared on Greek philosophy, especially the philosophy of Socrates, Plato, and Aristotle. As the Romans expanded their empire they were exposing many people to Greek philosophy as well as Greek scientific reasoning and the Greek mathematics of geometry.

As Aristotle had written, everything comes from something else, Note, here, his *"Process of Change."*

> Everything which comes into being is brought about by something, that is, by a source from which its generation comes. And it is composed of something. Now this latter is best described not as the absence of the thing but as the matter from which it comes. and it becomes a particular thing, as a sphere or a circle or some other thing. Now one does not "make" the material - as the bronze - of which a thing is composed; so one does not make

the sphere, except in a secondary sense, in so far as the bronze circle is a circle and one makes it. For the act of making a particular thing is a process of making it out of some material in general. I mean that to make the bronze round is not to make the "round" or the "sphere," but quite a different thing - that of putting this form into what did not make it previously. If one made the "form," one would make it out of something else, for this would underlie it, as when one makes a sphere out of bronze. This is done by making a particular kind of substance, namely bronze, a special sort of thing, namely a sphere. And if one makes this "sphere" also in the same way, it is evident that he will make it in the same manner, and the process of origination will go on to infinity. It is evident therefore that the form, or whatever one ought to call the shape of the perceived object is not "made." It does not "become" nor does it have an origin. Nor is there any for the essential conception of a thing. For this is what is implanted in another entity, either by training or by nature or by force. But one does cause the "bronze sphere" to be. For one makes it out of bronze and the form is "sphere." One puts the form into this matter, and it is then a bronze sphere. But if there is an origin for the "idea of sphere in general" it will be something generated from something else. That which is generated will have to be analyzed again in turn, and each reduced to something further, than that to something else; I mean in one aspect into matter, in another into form. A sphere is a figure whose surface is everywhere equally distant from a center. One aspect of it is the material into which the form is to be put; the other the form which is to be put into it. The whole is what results, namely, the bronze sphere.

It is evident from what we have said that the part which is spoken of as the form or the essence does not originate; but the combination which derives its name from this does; and in everything which originates there is matter, and it is now this thing, now that... Of things which come into existence some are generated by nature, some by art, some by chance. And all things which are generated are generated by something and from something and as some particular thing....

And so, Aristotle is saying that whatever exists was generated by something that existed before it. The existence, in THE GOLDEN AGE OF GREECE, of the desire for art, drama, philosophy, and science, lay dormant for many years after the collapse of the Roman Empire. During these many years of cultural darkness in the Medieval period there were philosophers and other men attempting in their own ways to define their period in history and the meaning of life for them at the time. But the pursuit of intellectual knowledge which had marked the years of Socrates, Plato, and Aristotle was replaced with the necessity to find ways to survive in perilous times.

We will not stop to study any philosophers during the Medieval Period until we get to the eleventh century when we will look at the philosophy of St. Thomas Aquinas. As you remember, the Medieval period was dominated by the church. Even so, there were many people questioning the faith. Aquinas brought these dissidents into the church's embrace, using Aristotle's logic in his efforts to prove the existence of God. To many people this seemed paradoxical because Aristotle cared nothing for religion. Aquinas, logically, took care of that in his reasoning.

Thomas Aquinas

1227-1274 A.D.

Italy

Though the church was the dominant political power in the Medieval period, there were people who questioned its basic philosophy and did not want to join the church. These people were called pagans. Also, there were people in this period who were becoming more interested in science, who could not reconcile science with religion. If these doubts had been permitted to grow unchecked, the Christian religion might have weakened to the point of disintegration.

St. Thomas Aquinas, who was made a Saint by the Catholic Church 50 years after his death has been credited with saving the Christian Church by using the scientific logic of Aristotle to explain the basis for belief in God, thereby bringing the scientifically minded back into the fold, and also giving the so-called pagans a reason to believe in a religion they had hitherto rejected. How and why did he do this?

Thomas Aquinas had been a religious youngster who, at the age of five, asked himself, "What is God?" He spent the rest of his life trying to answer that question.

Aquinas was born of a noble family. His father was the Count of Aquino and the count of two other districts in Italy. His mother was a noblewoman of Norman (French) descent. Thomas wanted to be a Dominican Friar, not a soldier as was expected of him. His family thought they could dissuade him from his religious inclination but they were unsuccessful. His brothers locked him up in the family castle for over a year, attempting to change his mind about his future. When he refused to agree to become part of the military nobility, they sent him "worldly" things to change his mind. These included spicy foods and romantic books. His continuance to refuse their wishes prompted them to try one more thing: they sent an attractive, seductive young lady to tempt him further. He is reputed to have taken a burning log from the fireplace, lunged at her, and burned a cross on the door. This convinced his mother of his seriousness and she helped him to escape. He made his way to Cologne where he studied under a Dominican professor and later became a priest.

He searched for the meaning of life in asking constantly, "What is God?" He answered that the goal of our existence is God, and this goal is not offered to us as a gift, but it is attained only by extreme effort.

In much the same way that Zoroaster questioned the purpose of evil, Aquinas asked, why does God allow evil? His answer was that evil does not stand alone, but it is an imperfect good. Good is a battle against evil, like the plant struggling through the soil so it can sprout into the beauty (good) of flowers and leaves.

What, then, he asked, is the purpose of suffering and pain? His answer -- without pain and suffering the world would have no meaning. Situations that are always good would be boring. (It was several centuries later that Sigmund Freud theorized that the two most intolerable conditions are guilt and boredom).

Aquinas' philosophy is most important because he gave religion a rational (reasoned) basis. He used Aristotle's logic to demonstrate his idea that if you begin with faith you arrive at knowledge. Knowledge, he said, is limited, so one must begin with some innate sense as the basis of reasoning.

Aquinas attempted to eliminate the emotional aspect of religion, claiming that religion and sound scientific thinking aided each other. He used Aristotle's step-by-step approach to arrive at conclusions, dressing Aristotle's technique in Christian theology.

Note in the following excerpt from the First Article of *Summa Theologica* how Aquinas uses the tools of logic to determine if one has free choice.

We Proceed thus to the First Article:- Objection 1. It would seem that man has not free choice. For whoever has free choice does what he wills. But man does not what he wills, for it is written (Rom.vii.19): For the good which I will I do not, but the evil which I will not; that I do. Therefore man has not free choice. Objection 2. Further, whoever has free choice has in his power to will or not to will, to do or not to do. But this is not in man's power, for it is written (Tom.ix.16): It is not of him that willeth - namely, to will - nor of him that runneth - namely, to run. therefore man has not free choice. Objection 3. Further, he is free who is his own master, as the Philosopher says. therefore what is moved by another is not free. But God moves the will, for it is written (Prov. xxi.1): The heart of the king is in the hand of the Lord; whithersoever He will He shall turn it; and (Phil. ii.13): It is God who worketh in you both to will and to accomplish. Therefore man has not free choice. Objection 4. Further, whoever has free choice is master of his own actions. But man is not master of his own actions, for it is written, (Jer. x.23): The Way of a man is not his, neither is it in a man to walk. Therefore man has not free choice. Objection 5. Further, the Philosopher says: According as each one is, such does the end seem to him. But it is not in our power to be such as we are, for this comes to us from nature. Therefore it is natural to us to follow some particular end, and therefore we are not free in so doing. On the contrary, It is written (Eccles.xv.14); God made man from the beginning, and left him in the hand of his own counsel; ....That is, in the liberty of choice....And so there is nothing in this that is repugnant to free choice.

Aquinas was criticized for bringing Aristotle's logic together with Christianity. Remember that Aristotle was born several hundred years before Christ and so would be considered a pagan by the Christians. Aquinas answered his critics by saying that if Aristotle had been alive during the time of Christ, he would have become a Christian.

JOHN LOCKE

1632-1704

England

Over a period of several hundred years, from the end of the Medieval period and into the Renaissance, the power of the church was gradually replaced by the power of kings warring against each other either to make their kingdoms more secure, or to acquire more territory.

John Locke, a medical doctor, and the son of an attorney, was seventeen years old when his country's tyrannical king, Charles I, was captured by Cromwell's army, tried for treason, and beheaded. When Cromwell seized power, he was expected to rescue the people from the cruelty of their king. Instead, as Locke realized, Charles I's tyranny was simply replaced by Cromwell's tyranny. Cromwell was joined by men who had been tormented under Charles I. They, then, became the tormentor and oppressors under Cromwell. It was a very emotional time for the people of England.

All of this political turmoil had a profound effect on Locke and was responsible for at least part of his great interest in the function of government. Probably more than any other person, John Locke is responsible for the Western world's shift from monarchies to democracies. That change in power, however, was not a reality until about one hundred years after Locke's death. But he started the trend of thought about an idea that had been practically ignored in history up until his time. He was concerned about the rights of the average person, something we have learned to take for granted.

Locke examined society's need for some kind of government. He compared a man in what he called "a state of nature," to a man in society. Man and his family, out in the wilderness, can survive by himself up to a point. He has only limited protection if attacked and he may easily be robbed of all his possessions. If he joins the society of others for his protection, he gains security but he loses a measure of his freedom. Locke felt that this was a fair exchange.

Having seen the effects of tyrannical non-representative government under Cromwell, Locke believed that the only good government was self-government where a group of men would choose a few men to rule the rest of the men and women. He said that the rulers should have only that power which the electorate gives to them, and if the chosen rulers usurp (exceed) the specific power given them, then the electorate has not only the right, but the duty to remove the rulers from office even if revolution is the only way to do it in order to preserve the government. Otherwise the rulers will have stolen more than was allocated to them, and are no better than the barbarian robbers in the "state of nature." All people, he said, even commoners, have the right to life, liberty, and their possessions. We will not get into a discussion here as to how his ideas related to women. For the most part, historically, women's rights have nowhere equalled whatever rights were achieved by men. But that's another story.

Governmental authority, Locke added, was only good if it was delegated by the subjects. It was a form of social contract between those who rule and those who put the rulers in office, and as a contract it was binding on rulers and subjects according to the agreed-upon terms.

In his *"Essay Concerning Human Understanding,"* he endeavored to discover the source of human knowledge. He denied Socrates' and Plato's idea that we hold within us all knowledge and that it is only a matter or recognizing or remembering it. Locke said, instead, that one's mind is like a sheet of white paper. The sensations acquired from experience give us the knowledge that is written on this paper.

Locke was one of the first men in what became known as THE AGE OF REASON. His ideas on the rights of the individual gave impetus to much thought and discussion on the condition of the common man. Heretofore, in history, the ordinary citizen had not been much in the mind of upper class men. But Locke started a new line of thought when he attempted to replace the divine right of royalty with what he felt was a more humane right - that of human justice.

He said that we all have within us an innate sense of justice. and NO person, (not even a ruler) knowing what is just, ought to treat another unjustly. Nor should one impose his or her opinion on another because no person, he said, has the evidence that what they believe is the truth. No one should shackle the thoughts of others. Prejudiced people, he said, are just as opinionated as those whose minds they would change. Of religion, he said that all men being born free should believe as they wish. This was a very liberal idea in his time, and indeed even in our own time.

Though Locke was an Englishman, his ideas were read and discussed on the continent of Europe and especially in the salons (parlors of private homes) in Paris. There, such men as Voltaire, Rousseau, and Diderot met with friends and talked about Locke's "revolutionary" idea that the common man was born with certain rights. The writings of Locke, Voltaire, and Rousseau affected the political history of France and the United States. The common people in both of these countries rose up in military revolution against their tyrannical rulers. And one can most certainly hear Locke's philosophy in both the Declaration of Independence and The Constitution of the United States. For instance, in the Declaration of Independence:

> We hold these truths to be self-evident, that all men are created equal, that they are endowed by their Creator with certain unalienable Rights, that among these are Life, Liberty and the pursuit of Happiness. That to secure these rights, Governments are instituted among Men, deriving their just powers from the consent of the governed. That whenever any Form of Government be-

comes destructive of these ends, it is the Right of the People to alter or to abolish it, and to institute new Government... when a long train of abuses and usurpations, pursuing invariably the same Object evinces a design to reduce them under absolute Despotism, it is their right it is their duty, to throw off such Government, and to provide new Guards for their future security....

In addition to looking at those important documents, let's look at some excerpts from Locke's *"Of Civil Government."*

Chapter VIII

Of the Beginning of Political Societies

Men being, as has been said, by nature, all free, equal, and independent, no one can be put out of this estate, and subjected to the political power of another, without his own consent. The only way, whereby any one divests himself of his natural liberty, and puts on the bonds of civil society, is by agreeing with other men to join and unite into a community, for their comfortable, safe, and peaceable living one amongst another, in a secure enjoyment of their properties, and a greater security against any, that are not of it. This any number of men may do, because it injures not the freedom of the rest; they are left as they were in the liberty of the state of nature. When any number of men have so consented to make one community or government, they are thereby presently incorporated, and make one body politic, wherein the majority have a right to act and conclude the rest.

Chapter IX

Of the Ends of Political Society and Government

If man in the state of nature be so free, as has been said: if he be absolute lord of his own person and possessions, equal to the greatest, and subject to nobody, why will he part with his freedom? Why will he give up his empire and subject himself to the dominion and control of another power? To which it is obvious to answer, that though in the state of nature he has such a right, yet the enjoyment of it is very uncertain, and constantly exposed to the invasion of others: for all being kings as much as he, every man his equal, and the greater part no strict observers of equity and justice, the enjoyment of the property he has in this state is very unsafe, very insecure. This makes him willing to quit a condition, which, however, free, is full of fears and continual dangers: and it is not without reason, that he seeks out, and is willing to join in society with others, who are already united, or have a mind to unite, for the mutual preservation of

their lives, liberties, and estates, which I call
by the general name, property.

FRIEDRICH WILHELM NIETZSCHE

1844-1900

Germany

You no doubt felt "at home" reading about John Locke because you have grown up with ideas on the rights of common people and ideas on government of and by the people. The philosophy of Nietzsche is a contrast to Locke's because it is contrary to what you have grown up with and therefore it may very possibly offend you. But that does not mean that you should not know about it. If people read, hear, or see only what they already know, they will live in a narrow world indeed. Some people choose that kind of comfort. But the purpose of this book is to expose people to the varieties of intellectuality. Nietzsche's philosophy is one of these varieties that presents "the other side" of several ideas you probably accept.

You may also dislike abstract art, or impressionistic music, or existentialism, or any number of ideas or creations. That does not mean you shouldn't observe and study them. It doesn't matter whether you like or dislike the contents of this entire study. But if you try to understand the reasoning or the purpose behind the efforts of the people who have made the results of their search visible or audible for the rest of us to consider, you may be greatly enriched.

It might be best in this short study of Nietzsche to meet his ideas "head on" and then take a short look at his personal life. First of all, Nietzsche believed that there were forces in the world which weakened human beings and prevented the development of great men. The villains for him were:

1. Democracies
2. Socialism or communism
3. Christianity

Democracy, he said, PRETENDS that people are equal. Socialism and communism cater to the taste of the masses, and Christianity preaches weakness. People who preach weakness are incapable of power. Why should everyone, he asked, do as Christianity preached and love his neighbor? (Incidentally Nietzsche was the son of a Protestant minister.)

He said that democracy, socialism, and Christianity SEEMED to be unselfish, but actually they are based on the resentment and the revenge that the weak people exercise over the strong as a kind of punishment by the weak. One should mistrust all in whom the impulse to punish is powerful. He said, too, that Christianity tames the heart, but that this is a mistake for there is superiority in a wild beast.

Christians, he said, love their enemies in this life so that they can go to heaven. It isn't that they REALLY love their enemies, he claimed. He attributed the rise of Christianity to a slave morality noting that it was the slaves and underprivileged who became the first Christians. He wrote, also, that people yearn for the after-life because they have failed in this life on earth.

The fact that not everyone can be rich, or intelligent, or powerful means that the masses of average people will pull down everyone else to their level. Workers resent the wealthy non-working people, and they resentfully attempt to reduce the power of the rich in the name of brotherhood.

In his writing, Nietzsche created a Superman who unabashed strives for power. While his writings were projected as philosophical ideas and were not written to put into effect, it is widely believed that dictators and other power-minded men like Hitler and Mussolini seized upon his ideas and used them as justification for their dictatorial and fascist actions.

The noblest occupation, Nietzsche said, is to wage war, and to kill in order to live. There was the justification that a war-monger could use! In the Noble Soul, he said, there is no resentment: there is a frank honest, sincere Will to Power, which is the title of one of his writings. Cruelty, he added, is the cardinal principle of man and one must be extremely cruel in order to be good. The strengths of the master class, he said, are ambition, ruthlessness, and hate. One can see in all of this how Hitler could have used these ideas to justify his actions.

After you have read the excerpt from Nietzsche's *The Will to Power* answer for yourself the questions: What is the herd morality and what are its most broadly preached doctrines? What are the con-

ditions in which Man can grow up most vigorously:
How does the herd morality prevent greatness?

> Section 957. It draws near, inexorable, trem-
> bling, as frightening as fate -- the great task
> and question, How shall the earth as a whole
> be administered? And toward what end shall
> mankind as a whole - no longer a mere
> people, a race - be trained and cultivated?
> Legislated morals are the chief means
> whereby one can cull from man what is
> suitable to a creative and profound will:
> provided that such a high order artist-will has
> power in hand and is able to impose itself
> over long periods in the form of lawgiving,
> religions, and moralities. To my mind, such
> men of great achievement, such authentical-
> ly great men, will be pursued in vain today
> and probably for a long time to come. They
> are lacking, and will be, until finally, after
> much disappointment, one begins to under-
> stand why they are lacking, and that now and
> for a long time to come nothing impedes their
> genesis and development with greater hos-
> tility that what passes in Europe for "the
> morality" - as though there were and could be
> no other - the one heretofore described as
> herd morality, the one which strives with all
> its might for that common green pasture-land
> happiness on earth, i.e., security, absence of
> danger; coziness, ease of life, and last but not
> least, "if all goes well," the pious hope of dis-
> pensing with all manner of shepherds and

bell-wethers. Its two most broadly preached doctrines are called "equality of rights" and "compassion for all suffering" - and suffering itself is thought to be something which must by all means be got rid of. That such ideas can still be modern inclines one to a low opinion of modernity. But whoever ponders thoroughly the question where and who the plant Man has hitherto grown up most vigorously cannot help but suppose that this occurred under quite the contrary conditions; that the danger of its habitat must be magnified to frightful proportions, its powers of sensation and locomotion must struggle against long hardship and constriction, its will to life must be intensified into unconditioned will to power and predominance, and that danger, harshness, violence, period in the street as in the heart, inequality of rights, concealment, stoicism, the art of seduction, deviltry of any kind - in short, that the elevation of the species Man demands the very antithesis of all herdlike wish-fulfillment. A morality with such opposite intentions, seeking to nurture man upwards instead of into the cozy and the mediocre, a morality seeking to nurture a ruling caste - the future lords of the earth - must, before it can be promulgated, introduce itself as though in league with prevalent moral law and in the guise of the latter's words and shapes. But that accordingly a number of provisional and diversionary tactics need be discovered and that, whereas the life-span of a man means next to nothing in face of the fulfillment of such protracted tasks and aims, above all else a new species must be nurtured, in which the appropriate wills and instincts will be guaranteed duration through many generations -a new ruling species and caste: to envision all this is no easier than to comprehend the lengthy and hard-to-articulate Etcetera of its underlying thought. To prepare a transvaluation of values for a certain powerful species of men, endowed with the highest intellect and willpower, and to this end liberate him slowly and carefully from a host of repressed and vilified instincts: who ponders this belongs to us, the free spirits....

Nietzsche examined Zoroaster's philosophy on the struggle between good and evil and re-wrote his interpretation into a highly imaginative and poetic book, *Thus Spake Zarathustra* (Zoroaster's Persian name). Nietzsche said that the world is a struggle of the greed of the masters who will triumph over the masses. Slaves should be exploited and many men must perish in order that Superman will live. The whole French Revolution was justified, he maintained, in that it provided the background and the action for the creation of the talents of Napoleon.

Superior people should resist the inroads that the masses make on their lives. He wanted an international ruling race and he would call them Lords of the Earth. How would this compare with Plato's philosophy of who should rule, or with Locke's?

Nietzsche could not be compassionate. He embraced the things he himself felt he did not have -- physical strength. His health was always poor and he was quite weak. He had suffered emotionally from the failure of a love affair.

Though he grew up in Prussia (the name of the country which became Germany), he did not like the Germans. He spent many years of his life in Switzerland and was for a time a professor in Basel, Switzerland until he retired early in life because of ill health. His last years were spent confined from society because he had gone insane.

Nietzsche had come from Germany, but he did not like what he felt was happening to that country. He saw that after it had unified that it had achieved power and security and that its soul was dead. He thought that nothing great was going to happen to it and he, in part, wanted to shock people to achieve greatness, and to turn their back on their cultural decadence.

EXISTENTIALISM

Kierkegaard, Sartre, Camus, Kafka, Becket

I would rather be ashes than dust:

I would rather my spark should burn out in a brilliant blaze than that it should be stifled in dry-rot.

I would rather be a superb meteor, every atom of me in magnificent glow, than a sleepy and permanent planet.

Man's chief purpose is to live, not to exist.

I should not waste my days trying to prolong them.

I shall use my time.

Jack London

This poem embodies an existentialist idea, and in reading it you can understand why existentialism is referred to as the "now" philosophy.

The existentialist philosophers say that up until now, philosophers have wasted their time searching for rational answers to the meaning of life and that life cannot be explained rationally, nor can one make any sense out of life as a whole.

The word, "existentialism," comes from the word, "exist." These modern philosophers say that we are "trapped" in existence, that we are living in a meaningless world. We cannot order our lives because the merest incident may change our whole life's scheme in an instant. But one thing is sure -- we have to deal with existence.

There are many philosophers who could be called existentialists, but probably the most well known are the ones listed at the beginning of this section. They vary according to their emphasis. Some believe in God and some do not. They all agree that the old traditional philosophies are remote from life. Typical of their time in history, the existentialists are in revolt and protest.

There are three main ideas which occur in the writings of these men, from time to time, and they have become the central points of existentialism:

1. Choice
2. Commitment
3. Responsibility

The first idea, choice, refers to our "awful" (meaning full of awe) freedom of choice. Everything we do is based on a choice we have made. Relating that to yourself, we could say that the fact that you are, at this moment, where you are, is the result of your choice. Students in school for instance may say that they HAVE to be in school and that they have no choice. But they have only to remember that many of their ex-school mates chose to drop out of school and to do other things, or to do nothing at all.

Students can say, too, that they are in school because their parents demand it. But they have only to recall that many other parents made the same demand on their sons and daughters who then chose to disregard their parents' demands. Following advice is a choice in itself; not everyone does. Many people trudge to boring jobs every day. They say they HAVE to work. But they don't have to. It is their choice. The alternative choice of not working is, for them, comparatively unattractive.

However, whatever the choice, there is no way for us to escape the consequences of our choice. And here is the second existentialist idea -- commitment. With the choice goes commitment to the choice, or doing that which you have chosen to do. The third idea, responsibility goes with living with the consequences of our choice. The existentialists say that the noble person takes the responsibility for his own choice.

And because people should be responsible for their choices, their alibis are unacceptable. If we are in a bad situation it is our own fault. Existentialists would say that no gods are responsible, no environment, no heredity, no race or caste, no parent, no wrong education, no teacher, no bad childhood situation, and no inner complex.

We do not have to stay in a bad situation. Having the "awful" freedom to choose, we suffer or are rewarded by the consequences. When things go wrong, it is too easy for us to blame someone or something else. Men and women rely on themselves. That does not mean that they should withdraw from their commitment to the world.

This particular concept of depending on ourselves is very similar to the Buddhist philosophy which stresses one's relying on one's self rather than on a god. Many people who do not know Buddhism, erroneously believe that Buddha is a god, but as he repeatedly stated, he was only a man, trying to get people to rely on themselves. Blaming others, the Buddhists believe, is an evasion of a person's responsibility of her or his freedom of choice.

The best that people can hope for in life, the existentialists say, is their dignity and nobility of their integrity, commitment, and responsibility to the choice they made.

But because life is unpredictable, and even absurd, people may be robbed of that dignity. From this philosophy, a new theme in playwriting developed as part of the existentialist movement, pointing up the absurdity of life, called relevantly, *"The Theatre of the Absurd."*

One of these existentialist plays, *"Waiting for Godot,"* by Samuel Becket, is about two men, who, throughout the play, wait for someone named Godot, who never arrives, pointing out our absurd plight of waiting for something that we are never sure of and which never comes.

In a short story by a writer named Sartre, entitled, *"The Wall,"* a prisoner of war defends a fellow soldier even unto death by not revealing the soldier's hiding place. But by an ironical choice that the defended soldier makes, the prisoner is robbed of the nobility of the responsibility and commitment of this choice. However, when the prisoner is released after having faced death squarely and nobly, he now sees life differently. It was Sartre who said, "Life begins on the other side of despair," and "We die alone, and to a certain extent we must live alone; all we really have is a fidelity (truthful loyalty) to ourselves."

A short novel, *The Stranger*, by another existentialist, Camus, takes the reader through many pages of a man's uneventful life. On the spur of the moment, and almost as a fluke, the man kills another man. He could probably have been acquitted of murder, but his prosecutors refer to and convict him on his past life. They bring into the case his seeming lack of concern for his mother's death at her funeral, his disinterest in any employment advancement, and his unemotional involvement with his girl friend.

It is because he has made a choice to live the way he believes that he must die. IF he had pretended to care about his mother's death, (which is at least the conventional thing to do) or take the job promotion offered to him, or told the girl he was going to marry that he loved her, which he didn't, he would have been living as other people wanted him to live.

The existentialists claim that nobility comes from one's honesty (integrity) to commitment. In *The Stranger*, the man could have saved his life, but he would have had to abandon his principles, his honesty, his integrity.

The person considered to be the forerunner of the recent existentialist philosophers was a writer in Denmark named Kierkegaard who wrote about 1850. One of his important theories was that learning takes place only when there is enlightenment. It is strange and even rather miraculous, this enlightenment. Almost a dawning, or a surprise realization of some knowledge that the learner did not have before. Ignorance of the subject is then replaced with knowledge and the learner is different than he or she was before. The more recent existentialist philosophers turned back to Kierkegaard and embraced many of the ideas of his philosophy as embodying the themes of their "now" philosophy.

SUMMARY

From the first readings in this study of Zoroaster, Socrates, Plato, and Aristotle, you have come "full around" back to Socrates at least. For it was Socrates who believed that philosophy should be a living part of one's life. Most of the philosophers between Socrates and the existentialists have been what we could call analytical or theoretical philosophers. They have tried out their ideas on paper. For the most part their ideas were not intended as what could be, but at the time of their writing, they were ideals only.

The existentialists have attempted to bring philosophy "down to earth." If we don't like their philosophy it may well be that we don't appreciate the answers to life's questions today that have been uncovered for us by the existentialists in their search for the meaning of life.

People search for the meaning of life through many avenues. Philosophy is one of these avenues. Religion, science, and the arts are other avenues. Let us see what religion has offered to people in the eastern and western parts of the world.

CHAPTER THREE

RELIGION

Religion in the Public Schools

Recently the San Francisco Chronicle published the following article:

Court's Ruling

Back-to-school time is an appropriate season to review a question on which vast confusion continues to exist throughout America: namely, what does the Constitution permit public schools to do, and what does it forbid them to do about religion?

James V. Panoch of the Public Education Religious Studies Center has compiled a brief, easy-to-comprehend list of do's and don'ts that deserves the attention of every school official, teacher, and parent.

Panoch cuts through all the jargon of court decisions and gets down to brass tacks: A public school 'may sponsor the study of religion, but may not sponsor the practice of religion.'

That is the key point which the Supreme Court tried to make in both of the two famous rulings which it handed down years ago about prayer and Bible reading in classrooms. The court did not -- as many critics have noisily protested -- 'ban God from our schools.' It did not 'outlaw' private, voluntary prayer. It actively encouraged objective study of the Bible as a tremendously important part of our heritage.

All it said was that a public school, as an official agency of government, has no constitutional right to conduct miniature worship services in the form of classroom 'opening exercises,' as thousands of public schools used to do every day.

The Supreme Court also went out of its way to urge schools to teach objective courss in comparative religion and the role that religious beliefs and organizations have played in history. Panoch neatly summarizes the court's basic rule for such studies:

'The public school may sponsor the study of religious views, but may not impose any particular view.'

'The school's approach in religion must be one of instruction, not indoctrination,' he said. 'The function of the school is to educate students about all religions, not convert students to any one religion. A school should strive for student awareness of all religions, but must not press for student acceptance of any religion.'

Even Russia, with its Communistic philosophy that denied the existence of God, and decreed that religion outside the home was illegal, has recently changed this stand, permitting public worship of religion. In the Soviet Republic of Georgia, there is a new course in the school system which teaches comparative religion, developed to give students a better understanding of their own history which was for many years interlaced with s-Christianity.

The Alexandria, Virginia based Association for Supervision and Curriculum Development in July, 1987, called for public schools to teach about religion, saying, "Religious education, or teaching of religion, is the job of parents and religious institutions, but teaching about religion is a legitimate purpose of public schools." The association added that art classes should include the effect of Christianity on Michaelangelo; world history courses should cover such topics as the rise of Christianity in the Roman Empire, the Crusades, the Reformation and the treatment of Jews and Moslems in the Spanish Inquisition; and literature students should read not only the Bible but passages from the Koran, the Gita, the Talmud and other sacred writings. "Because religion is so controversial a subject," the report said, "many educators have opted for benign neglect in their classrooms... The outcome has been massive ignorance of any faith besides one's own... a person cannot be fully educated without understanding the role of religion in history, culture and politics."

Then in June, 1988 fourteen religious and educational groups from the Americans United For Separation of Church and State and the National Association of Evangelicals issued a pamphlet with the hope that it will give teachers and principals courage to teach about religion in history, literature and other classes. "Failure to understand even the basic symbols, practices and concepts of the various religions," the pamphlet states, "makes much of history, literature, art, and contemporary life unintelligible." Other sponsors of the pamphlet encouraging the teaching of religion in the public schools include the National School Boards Association, the American Association of School Administrators, the Christian Legal Society, the National Conference of Christians and Jews, the National Council of Churches of Christ, the National Council for the Social Studies, the Association for Supervision and Curriculum Development, the American Federation of Teachers and the National Education Association.

Introduction

People search for explanations of their lives in many ways. As you have just read in the philosophy section, throughout history, we question and then we endeavor to answer our own questions. In philosophy, people have pondered, analyzed, and

answered questions that they have put before themselves time and time again. Through the use of
REASONING, philosophers have arrived at conclusions, whereas in religion, people have assumed
ON FAITH. Of course each religion has its own
philosophy, but each religion's philosophy is
grounded on faith.

The mysticism of religion has come down
through history stronger than any other force yet
known. Through the zeal of any number of different
religions, governments have toppled, lands have
been laid bare, people have moved from continent
to continent both in peace and in war in search of
religious freedom or new converts, or in religious
persecution, suppression, or domination. More
people have been slain in religious persecution than
for any other cause so far in history. Generally speaking, people have believed that their own religion is
good and any other religion is probably worthless or
possibly an affront to their own. But whatever the
result, good or bad, or whatever the philosophy of a
person's religion, or the course it has taken, one
thing has proved true -- most people need religion.

There are those who say this need for religion
is a human weakness, a "crutch" to lean on, and they
may be right. Most people do need some kind of a
"crutch" no matter what they call it. But the critics of
religion need to be reminded that though religious
zeal has led to murderous assaults, it has also been
the most consistent social force operating to bring
out the unselfish qualities in people and to restrain
acquisitive and greedy instincts.

Though religion, through most of its history has been a force for good behavior, it actually probably began for very different reasons. Prehistoric people had much to fear. For one thing, there were all those unknown forces controlling the weather which in turn controlled life, food supply, and as they believed, the birth and death of loved ones and enemies. Early tribal people tried to appease these powers, these gods, for their own protection and well-being. So it was most likely out of fear that people first worshipped something stronger than themselves.

As people joined into groups which became tribes, the smart person in the group who could learn to predict the unknown forces like weather, or death, or birth, appeared therefore to control these things. This intelligent and clever person came to be either a god or goddess or at least a go-between, a Priest or Priestess or a Shaman who could easily gain power over the tribe.

Those people closest to understanding uncontrollable powers were the best able to control other people. Quite naturally this kind of power was abused, for nothing corrupts a person faster than power. But this power was good, too. In order for people to live together they had to agree to certain rules. These rules could come from a group of people and they could come from the supernatural, as unseen powers are reputed to have sent messages to earth many times for people to live in peace together.

Religion as one of the controlling forces of humankind has, in many cases, been much stronger than civic law because religion appeals to one's conscience. There is a current and prevalent conception that if a person breaks a law it is a sin only if the person gets caught. If one's crime goes undetected or if a person is acquitted, it is as though she or he committed no wrong. Not so with religion. The courtroom of one's conscience forgives grudgingly, if at all. So one can see how valuable it is for governmental leaders to have their subjects believe, not only in the law, but also in a religion. This gives the leaders two sources of power to rely on. And power is not necessarily bad. As religion especially is a power encouraging the morality of men and women, then it must be considered a great force for the good of human beings. Will Durant has written in *The Lessons of History* that there is no important example in history of a society effectively sustaining moral life without the help of religion.

But why does religion seem to be necessary to encourage one to be good? Left to one's own merits, would one do good rather than bad? In his *Lessons of History* Durant provides his answer to that question when he says that he doesn't know what the heart of a bad person is like, but he says he DOES know what's in the heart of an honest man and it is TERRIBLE.

What of places and people who don't have religions, communist countries for example? It has been said that communism itself is a religion. It has all the essentials: a leader, a book to follow, a philosophy, rituals, and it has attendance that is required at its ceremonies. It is, therefore, a political religion.

Some people might shudder to hear that religion and politics have similarities and yet the fact that they are both based on faith is probably the reason why there exists the old adage, "When you're in polite society, never argue about religion or politics." It is difficult to argue away another person's faith.

It was Mahandas Ghandi who said that anyone who thought religion and politics were separate things did not know what they were talking about.

He called upon the religion of the Hindus to achieve political freedom for his people from the British.

In our own country, our governmentally printed money says, "In God We Trust." Most of our leaders are sworn into office with their hands on the Bible. It is as though there could be a tinge of treason ascribed to a leader who did not believe in Christianity, in spite of the base of religious toleration on which our country was founded. But this is all to say that though we try to separate church and state, they exist as partners in social control. People have needed both powers.

Back to the question of the necessity for religion, other than the fact that societies have needed it. Why have individuals so readily and continuously accepted something they cannot see? Many thoughtful people have wondered about the worship of the mystical. The world famous historian, Toynbee, has said that there is a presence in the universe that is greater than man himself. Another explanation for the need for religion is offered by the psychiatrist Freud, who has said that this need is related to the infant's feeling of helplessness and the need for a father's protection. (Freud ignores goddess worship.)

Jung, another psychiatrist, said that one's mental health depends on exercising one's religious function. Tremendous temples, shrines, and cathedrals throughout the world are manifestations of this function. If one loses faith in religion, Jung says, one often transfers that exercise of religious function to other areas of interest. People who are zealously involved in ecology, or consumer protection, or fighting communism, or helping the poor people, or enthusiastically pursuing any specific interest, may be spending their religious fervor in that direction while others spend theirs in church worship. But Jung would say that no matter how it is used, the religious function is a necessary action for a mentally healthy person.

Goddess Worship

That women were responsible for religious and priestly purposes in pre-Greek cultures is attested to by many, including the Swiss historian, Johann Bachhoven, from his archaeological discoveries of mother-right societies. There was, as he said, a "world view" around the Great Goddess. The "all-mother", he and others claim, is older than "the all-father."

Because women could bring forth human life, it was believed they were responsible for all life - plants and animals - even for night and day. In the Russian Ukraine as early as 30,000 B.C. there is evidence that worshipers gathered to honor the goddess. Each city-state in ancient towns worshiped their own particular gods and goddesses and temples were erected to each. Priests and priestesses served the gods and goddesses.

As quoted in *Women's Roots*, the principal deities of Babylonia were the god Marduk and the goddess Ishtar known previously as Inanna and later as Astarte to the Greeks and Ashtoreth to the Jews. Among other Babylonian gods were Anu, Shamash, Nannar, and Baal. Marduk, however, assumed his supremacy.

Whereas goddesses had represented abundance from the earth, male gods functioned from the sky. Tribal, Egyptian and Greek gods had wives or consorts. The male god of Israel, Yahweh, or Jehovah, was exclusively male with no female consort. From then on, western religion is patriarchal.

Early Judaism put an end to goddesses, established a single, male divinity, established the Ten Commandments which are the basis of moral, social life in the Western Hemisphere, and through the Adam and Eve myth explained sin as the primal transgression of man against God, instigated by women.

Western Religions

Originated in the Near East, but moved primarily into the Western World -- also known as Occidental

Judaism

Belief in one God. Religion of the Jews, also known as Hebrews.

Christianity

Belief in one God and in Jesus Christ as the Messiah. Many sects of Christianity believe in the Holy Trinity (Father, Son, and Holy Spirit)

Islam

Belief in one God, Allah. This religion also known as Moslem, Muslim, Mohammedism, Muhammedism.

Eastern Religions

Originated in the Far East, India and China, and practiced predominantly in the Eastern or Oriental world.

Hinduism

Belief in many gods and goddesses

Buddhism

Belief in no god - originally.

The originators of the Western religions were the Jews: the originators of the Eastern religions of Hinduism and Buddhism were the Indians of India.

Four Things Typical of Western Religions

1. Each claims to be the direct revelation of the one true God.
2. Revelation is the method by which God makes Himself known. His sovereignty is absolute.
3. This life is a person's only life and cannot be repeated on earth.
4. Earthly life is a very serious affair and a person will be held accountable to God for what he does on earth.

Two Things Typical of Eastern Religions

1. No clear conception of God as Lord
2. Self-improvement or self-ascendency (transcending one's body) is of greater concern than worship of a kind of god or idol.

We in the Western world have seen a great deal of religious competition. In each town of any size we see many different churches with varying philosophies, each claiming to be the best for its worshipers. This is said to be representative of the extrovert and somewhat aggressive personality of the Western world as compared to the Eastern world which is seen as more passive and introspective. Religions reflect these personalities. Even so, the religions all have a lot in common as we can see in similarities to the Christian Gold Rule:

The Golden Rule

ZOROASTRIANISM

Whatever is disagreeable to yourself, do not do unto others.

HINDUISM

Good people proceed while considering what is best for others is best for themselves.

BUDDHISM

Hurt not others with that which pains yourself.

JUDAISM

And thou shalt love they neighbor as thyself.

CHRISTIANITY

Therefore all things whatsoever ye would that man should do to you, do ye even so to them.

ISLAM

No one of you is a believer until he loves for his brother what he loves for himself.

   The earliest religion we will study briefly here is Hinduism.

HINDUISM

There is no word for religion in Hinduism. The word which is used means right, duty, good works. Hinduism is so old that it cannot be dated, nor can its beginnings be attributed to any person's teachings. The basic philosophical faith, or sdogma, of Hinduism, which originated in India and grew out of the Ancient Upanishad religion based on the old Vedic myths, is that the soul migrates from life to life and does not find its rest until it achieves Nirvana, or an ultimate union with the Universal Soul, called Brahman.

The soul's journey is governed by the law of Karma. This is the principle that says that the deed follows the doer. If one does bad things in this life, one's soul will suffer in some future life. If one does good deeds in this life, one's soul will have an easier time of it in the next life, or in a subsequent life.

Karmic action is a form of justice, coming from unseen, unheard forces. Everything one does is imprinted on one's soul, which may have been through thousands of lives before this one.

The Caste System

Another part of the dogma which is directly related to Karma is the principle of the caste system. In its recorded beginnings about 2000 B.C. in India, though in actuality it probably dates much further back, the caste system was a device to keep the invading Aryans from marrying outside their group, so as not to diminish their strength. It eventually became built into the religion by those who wanted to justify a superiority over others. Since Medieval times, the caste system has been based on birth. One is born into a caste and during one's lifetime there is no way to rise about the caste of one's birth.

Though there are five castes, each caste has been broken down to many sub-castes until there are well over 3000 castes, all more or less within the five major castes which include:

1. The priests - Brahmans (not to be confused with Brahman the Universal Soul.
2. The government administrators or soldiers -- Kahatriya
3. The craftsmen - Vaisya
4. The laborers - Shudra
5. The Untouchables or outcastes - Harijans

Even though, through the efforts of Mahandas Ghandi, Untouchability is illegal, it still operates because it is very difficult to legislate against religious tradition. The Hindus rarely marry outside their caste and most if not all of their social contacts are within their own caste.

There are many stories most likely true, and intriguing to the Westerner about Untouchability. The Untouchables are said to defile (dirty to the point of pollution) whatever and whomever they associate with. One story is written of an upper caste woman who saw her child fall into a river. An Untouchable offered to dive in and save the child, but the mother refused the offer because her child would have been defiled and it would be better off dead.

No matter how well an Untouchable succeeds, he or she is still an Untouchable. The Indian Constitution has made Untouchability illegal and the British opened up schools to them. Recently an Untouchable who graduated from law school (a very rare thing) was elected by the masses of Untouchables. In parliament he cannot overcome his caste. Though he dresses in clean western clothes and votes on legislation and is not sweeping the streets in rags, he is still considered an Untouchable. The mystique of religion is stronger than the law. And before we become too critical of this we must remind ourselves of our own treatment of Blacks and other minorities. No matter how much a Black or a Mexican, or a woman succeeds, each is still treated by many of his or her colleagues as an inferior. It is difficult to legislate morality too.

Reincarnation

Under the law of Karma, one is born into a caste as the result of what the owner of his or her soul did in a past life. If one is a Brahman (and only men can become Brahmans) he would know that whoever had his soul before he did, had done good deeds. If one is an Untouchable, the Hindu believes this low status is the result of wrong doing of the soul in another life. All of this is carried over into the whole world of life. A bug's soul belonged to a terrible person. If one does very bad things, at death this soul may inhabit the soul of a newborn pig. Here from the Hindu religion, *The Garuda Purana* explains the Hindu acceptance of Karma:

> Our life comes from the unseen and goes to the unseen. Its middle part only being manifest. What is there to mourn for in this?

> A man dies not before the appointed time, even if he is riddled with shafts. A wound from the tip of a Kusa sprout proves fatal at the right moment. A man receives that which he is fated to receive, goes only there where fate leads him, and finds only that much pleasure or pain which he is destined to meet in this life. What is there to mourn for in this life?

> Flowers bloom and fruits ripen in their appointed time and of their own accord without waiting for anybody's bidding: and the effects

of one's Karma bide their time and become patent only on the right occasion. Birth, education, conduct, character, virtue, or connection avails not a man in this life. The effects of one's Karma and penance, done in prior existence, fructify, like a tree, at the appointed time in the next.

The Karma of a man forcibly draws him to the place where death or fortune waits him. The effects of deeds one by a man in a prior existence overtake and choose him out of the next, as a calf finds its own mother out of a thousand cows. Thus one's Karma binds one for good or evil. Pleasure or pain, happiness or misery, is the direct result of one's good or bad deeds in a prior birth. Why do you make such heavy stock of misery out of it, O you foolish one?

We in the Western world have looked on reincarnation with a certain humor because we don't believe it and we have no faith in it. We have seen it as an improbable but hypothetical opportunity to repeat our life in a more advantageous form on earth. The Hindu does not look on it as an opportunity. Hindus live in fear of being reborn. Their thrust in life is to lead such a good life that their Karma at death will be good enough to achieve Nirvana. This is an example of a power of religion helping people to live peacefully and morally with each other.

Nirvana

Nirvana is the Hindus' goal. It is the putting an end to the soul's journey in the cosmos. Hindus definitely do not want to be reincarnated because, they say, it is pointless. While we might say with good humor that reincarnation would give us a second chance, the Hindu asks, "Why keep the Wheel of Samsara forever turning -- the wheel of birth, old age, suffering, death, rebirth, old age, suffering, and death?"

In India, death is looked on with some joy because all who die, and all who loved the deceased, hope that at death the deceased's soul will come to its final rest and achieve Nirvana. It is the hope of the Hindu that at death the soul will unite with Brahman. (Though the world "Brahman, in this case is the same word as the word defining the caste of priests, when used in achieving Nirvana, "Brahman" has another interpretation.

It is at the river Ganges where millions of faithful Hindus have come to die, to be released from the cycle of rebirths, to achieve Nirvana. Their bodies are cremated in the ghats and their ashes taken to the river. The Ganges is considered the world's holiest river. To millions, Ganga, as it is called, is literally a God. Even if one is not going there to die, the Hindus who can, visit Ganga each morning as the sun rises, in what is known as the babyhood of the sun, they swim in its water which they consider to be swimming in the womb of God, and drink from the water that includes the ashes and bones of cremated bodies. Though many know scientifically that the water is polluted, they swim and bathe daily because not to do so would be to renounce their faith.

India's government has tried in many ways to clean up the Ganges River, to build sewage treatment plants to process the huge flow of waste water that pours into the river from major cities, to build electric crematories to replace wood pyres on which the approximately 42,000 bodies are burned which in turn produce 5000 tons of ashes. But all environmental efforts collide with religious tradition. There are people who cannot afford the traditional funeral rites, who dump their relatives' bodies into the river without burning. Then, also, according to the religion, a person who has died as a leper or from snakebite cannot be burned. His body must be dumped in the river whole. Even men of science, who work to clean up the river, bathe in it each morning, and drink its water, which they believe is holy.

Meditation and Yoga

Brahman is not God, nor a Supreme Being. It is the Impersonal Soul of the World. To achieve union with the Soul of the World, Hindus must have lived very moral lives. There are some very religious Hindus who attempt to achieve Nirvana, or this Union with Brahman in a state of selflessness, during their lifetime through Yoga. This is a practice of controlling their breathing, posture, and thought in meditation in order to escape their body, to transcend the worldly, and to attain a state which is physically and mentally unrelated to the senses, but related to a universality, a being at peace or at one with the universe.

Yoga, which means "union," is one of the many aspects of Eastern religion which is foreign to Western religions.

We see pictures of Hindu men practicing Yoga, their thin bodies contorted, some with their legs wrapped around their necks, and we wonder what that has to do with religion. But there are rituals that we in the Western world go through which puzzle the Easterner. In any study of religion, as in the study of any subject which shows us differences in the world, it is important to look openly and non-critically. True, this is easier said than done. When we choose to criticize those who are different from us, we close our minds to understanding and thereby cut ourselves off from wisdom. But if we are unable to look at others non-judgmentally, can we look at ourselves with anything but prejudiced self-righteousness?

Being specific, when references are made to the Hindu practice of Yoga, or their practice of worshipping the cow, we Westerners are inclined to scoff. From our viewpoint these practices are difficult to understand. Yet the Hindu feels it is just as reasonable to protect and feel affection for the cow, as many people do in other countries for their horses or dogs. It just happens that the Hindu mythology connotes deism or godliness to their cows. To argue with their belief is futile.

The worship of the cow, and even of monkeys and snakes, as sacred animals and reptiles, grows out of the philosophy of Karma and reincarnation that says there is no difference between the soul of an animal and the soul of a man. The body may be different but the soul is the same.

Hindu Gods and Goddesses

In addition to the life-long hope of achieving Nirvana and uniting one's soul with Brahman, the principal focus of Hindu worship is on three Gods, though there are over thirty million). These three Gods are:

Brahman (not to be confused with Brahman, the caste of priests),the giver of life;
Vishnu, the preserver of life;
Shiva, or Siva, the destroyer of life. Shiva destroys in order to rebuild. Eastern religions face the problem of death as a necessary part of new life, new thought, and other beginnings in the cycle of all the universe.

Hindus may worship one or all of these Gods and they worship in separate temples dedicated to the individual God. A person may have a favorite God and worship at that particular God's temple most of the time, or they may vary their place of worship and the God they wish to worship. Temples are erected and maintained by the people in the community and there is no church organization. Priests live from the gifts of people.

Conclusion

A lot of what the Western world knows about Hinduism has come from the writing of the Bhagavad Gita, the mythology which evolved from the Vedic myths. Much of the Buddhist mythology is also based on the *Bhagavad Gita.* In the same way as Judaism is the basis for Christianity, Hinduism is the basis for Buddhism.

Any study of Buddhism is first a study of Hinduism because the faith of many Buddhist sects is based on some elements of Hinduism. Though Buddhism originated in India about 500 B.C. and was very strong there for awhile, Hinduism again flourished, outlasting the missionary attempts not only of Buddhism, but also of Islam and Christianity. Hinduism has outlasted those who would criticize it, change it, or obliterate it. Hinduism has proved to be stronger than any of the governments of India, which have come and gone. As the historian, Will Durant says, India is Hinduism.

BUDDHISM

In a country north of India, Nepal, where Hinduism flourished, a young Hindu prince, Sakyamuni Gautama, the historical Buddha, grew up in wealth and comfort. (The historical Buddha is fictionalized in Herman Hesse's novel, *Siddhartha* Sakyamuni was born in 563 B.C. and after his lengthy princely training he married a lovely young woman, and a son was born to them. The prince seldom wandered outside his palace, but when he did he was distressed greatly by the suffering he saw among the poor people. He couldn't help but make a comparison between the life of poverty and anguish he saw outside his palace walls and his own lavish comfort. He wondered why there was so much suffering. Even at death, the souls of the sufferers would find no peace because their religion, Hinduism, told them that their souls would inhabit the body of another living person or creature and would suffer the same pain in the next life, going through a painful birth, then old age, and then death, only to be reborn again.

The prince, in wanting to search out the meaning of life that needed to be repeated over and over again, made a surprise move. He walked away from his palace one day, leaving his wife, his son, and all his luxury behind him, setting out in a six year's search, subjecting himself to starvation, mortification of the flesh, and constant wandering. He discussed the meaning of life and religion with any who would talk with him. To make a long story short, one time when he was sitting under the now famous Bo Tree in Central India, where he had been meditating for three weeks, he received what he called "Enlightenment." The name, "Buddha," means, "The Enlightened One."

His Enlightenment revealed to him that the Wheel of Samsara, which is the repetition of birth, old age, death, rebirth, over and over again, could be stopped in each life time so that a soul would not have to undergo reincarnation if a person could achieve a state of selflessness or Nirvana, by following a path of action that he outlined.

In Sarnath, India, he set out to preach what he had learned. This was the birth of Buddhism. On that day he had five disciples. Today there are five hundred million Buddhists. In many ways, Buddha's life paralleled that of Christ, though they lived at different times in history. They both wandered in poverty and they offered their religion to peoples of all walks of life

Ancient records indicate that Buddha's remains were first divided among eight Indian states after his cremation. Then Chinese records tells us that Indian monks brought 53 pieces of Buddha's remains, known as religious relics to China, and three were given to a temple near Beijing in the year 616 of the Chinese lunar calendar. The relics were undisturbed until 1592, when the empress had them placed in a white jade casket and placed in a cave near the Yunju Temple, on Shinjing Mountain where they remained until they were discovered in 1981 and verified as to their authenticity. The relics are known as sartras and "Are the only preserved sartras that we know of still extant in the world," according to Zhou Shaoling, deputy director of the Chinese Buddhist Association. The relics are two tiny brown pellets of ash, each the size of a small grain of rice. The only other remains of Buddha are two teeth, one housed in a temple on the outskirts of Beijing, and a second preserved in Sri Lanka, according to Zhou.

Buddhism Breaks With Hinduism.

In three ways Buddhism differed from Hinduism.

1. Release from the transmigration of the soul
2. Release from the caste system
3. Release from the dependence on gods, transferring that responsibility to the self.

In Hinduism men and women have prescribed duties in each stage of their lives and only when the family responsibilities are completed are they really free to renounce their worldly life and spend their time in meditation. Buddha, however, left his home as a young, married man, leaving his family responsibilities behind. He taught that attachment caused desire and desire caused suffering. The only true renunciant is one who owns nothing and is attached to no one.

Buddhist Belief

The Buddhists say that no one is responsible for you. You are responsible for yourself. If things do not go well for you, you have only yourself to blame. You cannot blame any god, or your parents, or a counselor who guided you, or your friends, or your environment.

In the same way, existentialists say that people are responsible for their own predicament, success or failure, happiness or unhappiness. Both existentialism and Buddhism have been considered to be initially depressing philosophies without the idea of salvation found in other philosophies and religions. Both, however, rest their hope in people which may be ultimate optimism.

As there is no caste system in Buddhism, any poor person can worship in a Buddhist temple, as their temples are open to all. This is not true in Hinduism, as the Untouchable caste could not enter a Hindu temple. Unlike the other major religions, Buddhism has no god, and Buddha himself said that he was only a man. In later years, however, the followers ascribed deism (godism) to Buddha, which he himself denied. His followers eventually even went so far as to evolve a series of saints or Bodhissatvas, men who had achieved Enlightenment and then spent their lives helping others achieve Enlightenment.

Buddha did not believe in a god. He said that people are in control of themselves and responsible for themselves. No man-created god was more powerful than a person. Within every person there is the potential to become a Buddha (to become Enlightened) to achieve selflessness and compassion, but one must work at it to invoke it for themselves.

The Four Noble Truths

The Buddhist who seeks Enlightenment must ascribe to the Faith of the Four Noble Truths which came to Buddha in his Enlightenment:

1. All life involves suffering.
2. All suffering is caused by desire and a wanting to hang on to permanence.
3. One can put down suffering by eliminating desire.
4. One does that by following the eight-fold path.

The Eight-Fold Path

1. Right Understanding
2. Right Thought
3. Right Speech

4. Right Action
5. Right livelihood
6. Right Effort
7. Right Mindfulness
8. Right Concentration.

Meditation

Both the Buddhists and the Hindus attempt to achieve a state of selflessness through Yoga or meditation. Through the repetition of the melodic "OM," or a Sutra, which is a few lines from the *BAHAGAD-GITA*, worshippers, after some practice, can mentally lift themselves out of the realm of space or time, or even away from their own sensations. They are then beyond desiring anything.

There are nine planes of meditation. When a Buddhist has achieved the ninth plane, "there is true self-conquest, and self-development." On the ninth plane there is no more hatred, no more desire, no confusion. There is unshakable truth. It is said to be, by those who have experienced it, an unspeakable bliss for the here and now, and not a kind of heaven that a morally good person will enter only when she or he dies.

Reality Vs. Illusion

The Buddhists believe that the state of self-lessness which one might attain with meditation is the "real" reality of life. But they make a distinction between reality and illusion that is difficult for the

Western mind to grasp. They say that whatever we perceive as real is actually an illusion, and that which we think of as an illusion is in fact reality. To take a Western approach to explain this, let us say that since everything is in a state of change, nothing really exists. For instance, you at this moment are changing, your cells are changing. The chair you're sitting in is deteriorating, slowly to be sure, but deteriorating nevertheless.

TIME is the vehicle which eventually changes everything. All things are in a state of change. Some things change faster than others, but everything changes. Therefore, the Buddhist philosophy says, the chair is really only an illusion of the chair, the apple is an illusion, the child, an illusion. And if that is true, what, then is reality?

Reality is what we think of as an illusion. Can you think of one? This is a difficult concept for the Westerner who is trained to think in terms of concrete examples, and to value THINGS more than THOUGHT. But when Buddhists can meditate to the point where they are in tune with the entire changing cosmos and UNITE THEIR OWN CHANGING PROCESS TO THE CHANGING COSMOS, they have attained a state of selflessness which is termed Nirvana. This is the ultimate in both Hinduism and Buddhism.

The Westerner has mistakenly confused the meaning of this word, "Nirvana," with some sense of ultimate sensual delight, but that interpretation would be one hundred percent wrong because in a state of Nirvana, one has transcended one's own senses and is not even aware of the sensual existence of one's own body.

Conclusion

As a social force operating for the moral good of its community, Buddhism offers this code: When one is about to do something, one should ask whether it will hurt self, hurt others, hurt both.

Anything harmful to another must not be done. The responsibility for good moral conduct and for freeing one's self from the Wheel of Samsara is the person's responsibility. "Buddha points the way: it is for you to swelter at the task."

Since, as the Buddhists believe, one does not owe his or her existence to a Creator God, or a master puppeteer, there is "no point in waiting for destiny, no point in performing rites, or praying, or imploring mercy or grace of a savior." Both the existentialist philosophers and the Buddhists make a person responsible for one's self.

Buddhism denies the existence of a god. Its dogma is to do away with reincarnation, to put an end to the Karmic action of one's soul now, not at death. And if one follows the right path for good moral conduct one will achieve their own reward -- especially if one does not desire it.

JUDAISM

The history of Judaism, a religion which began somewhere in the fertile crescent in the Near East, is the religion of the Jews, otherwise known as Hebrews of the Semitic group. The Semitic people, possibly after several droughts, moved in search of a better place to grow their crops. All of this would have been about 2000 B.C. and would have been at the same time the accounts of Hinduism in India were being recorded. When the Semites crossed over into Egypt, they were made the slaves of the Egyptians, a bondage that is presumed to have lasted from about 1500 to 1220 B.C.

Moses

A leader of the Egyptians, concerned with the treatment of the Semitic slaves who believed in one God and not many gods as the Egyptians did, learned that he was actually a Semite by birth. He eventually managed to get his people freed and across into the Sinai Desert. That man's name was Moses and the exit of the Jews from Egypt is known as "The Exodus."

On Mt. Sinai, Moses, the teacher of the Jews, is said to have seen God's message revealed or emblazened on the wall of a cave. This is what is meant by a religion of revelation. This revelation marks the beginning of Judaism. After Moses received the word of God in Sinai, he led them to the borders of the promised land, Jerusalem, but he died before he reached that destination.

The Torah

Moses gave the Jews the *Torah*, which is the first five books of the Old Testament of the Bible. *Torah* means "the law." Speculation on the origin of the *Torah* has filled thousands of books and we'll not go into that here. Suffice it to say, it is Jewish law and as the first five books of the Bible, is part of Christianity. Because Judaism and Christianity both use the Old Testament, it would be as difficult to separate some aspects of Judaism and Christianity, as it would be to separate some aspects of Hinduism and Buddhism, or for that matter, some aspects of Catholicism from Protestantism. As Aristotle said, everything comes from something else and retains something of its precedent qualities. The *Talmud,* is the interpretation of the *Torah.*

Saul, David, Solomon

In 1020 B.C. the Jews chose Saul as their king, but he led his people into a war with the Philistines where the Jews were severely defeated. Israel's ideal king was David. He conquered Jerusalem and led his nation to strength. David's son, Solomon (961 B.C.), the next king, built the first temple and was considered the wisest of men. Then in 722 B.C. the Kingdom was destroyed by the Assyrians, and in 586 B.C. the Jews were defeated by the Babylonians and taken into exile.

The Babylonian Exile

The significance of the Babylonian Exile is that this is the time and the place that the Jews must have come to realize that their chances of ever having a homeland would be slight. What would they have as a people if they had no country? This was the "odd" group in the vast Near East who believed in ONE God, Yahweh, later known as Jehovah, when all their neighbors believed in many gods. The Jews were different and they refused to change or to lose their identity by melding into other religions and losing their own. They were unshakable in their belief and for this it is said they have been to this day persecuted and destroyed. True, they were persecuted because some said they were guilty of Christ's death, but they were persecuted before the birth of Christ.

In the Babylonian Exile they found their strength and continuing unity in their *Torah*. It became a "portable homeland." It was at this time that the rabbi, the religious leader, became more important as a teacher of the Torah. Also, it was during the Babylonian Exile that centers for studying and perpetuating the religion were built. These were called synagogues. However, the most important center for religious worship was and is in the home.

Jewish Persecutions

Since the Babylonian Exile, the Jews have wandered the globe, being driven from place to place. During the Spanish Inquisition the enemies of Judaism destroyed the precious scrolls of the *Torah* and the *Talmud* as punishment for not converting to Christianity. When the Islamic religion became powerful in lands where Jews lived, they were tolerated for awhile, but when Mohammed realized that they were not going to join his new religion, he massacred them. Mohammed's successors allowed the remaining Jews to live, but they had to pay heavy taxes, as did the Christians. It was only after World War II, after six millions Jews had been exterminated by the Nazis, that Jerusalem and the country of Israel were given to the Jews, as a homeland. This meant that the Palestinian Arabs who lived there had to be displaced. Since 1946 these displaced Palestinians have lived in settlement camps set up by the United Nations. The political problems that this arrangement wrought have produced almost continuous war between the Palestinians and the Israelis.

What is a Jew?

The answer is that he or she is anybody who believes in the Jewish religion, in one God, Yahweh, or Jehovah. The Jews have no intermediary between God and humanity as the Christians have in Christ. Unlike the Christians, Jews do not believe that the savior of the people, the Messiah, has yet come. The Christians believe that Jesus is the Messiah who has come and that Jesus is the son of God.

The Jews have no church organization. A rabbi is anybody who wants to teach others the religion. In addition to *The Torah* and the *The Talmud*, which is the interpretation of *the Torah*, there is the *Mitzvot* which is the 613 Commandments for the moral conduct of a Jew. When a boy turns thirteen years old he is *Bar - Mitzvad*, which means he is now ready to take the adult responsibilities of synagogue participation.

The *Old Testament* of the *Bible*, written by prophets and religious leaders, is the history and thought of Judaism. It combines poetry, philosophy, and legend and laces it all together with a high moral purpose. Many of its ideas have carried through into Christianity, especially the idea of justice and reward for leading a good life and some kind of punishment for sin. It was a similar system of reward and punishment which helped the Christians in the long run, triumph over the Romans.

While Christianity stresses life after death in heaven or hell, Judaism is related more to the here and now. Both the Jews and the Buddhists stress the here and now and relate heaven and hell more to life on earth than the Christians do.

In the same way as the other major religions endeavor to invoke the goodness in humanity, Judaism to a great degree expects its adherents to care about humankind. Because they have been victims of persecution from their beginnings, they have, throughout their history, worked to help each other. "Helping others", is built into the creeds of most religions. But the Jewish faith carries the essence of helping and giving into its creed that the only true gift is an anonymous gift.

Following are several excerpts relating to religious persecution. This particular persecution victimizes Jews. There are numerous cases throughout history of one group's inhumanity to another group, manifested in the intolerance of religious beliefs. These particular excerpts are from the book, *The Source*, by James Michener. Permission to reprint these passages here has been granted by Random House, Inc. and Alfred A. Knopf, Inc., publishers of *The Source*.

The first passage describes a crusade as it is getting ready to leave an area in what is now Germany to travel to Jerusalem to rescue the Holy Land from the infidels.

The next weeks were filled with unusual activity. If Count Volkmar of Gretz was going to Jerusalem along with more than a thousand of his people, he would leave little to chance. For his wife and daughter, eight wagons and sixteen draft horses were provided filled with enough equipment to serve them and the six servants who would care for them. Eight additional wagons carried foodstuffs, implements and armor. Besides the servants for the countess, an even dozen serfs marched on foot to care for the count and Wenzel of Trier. In addition, eight grooms brought along some two dozen riding horses for the minor knights associated with the count, and these were followed by about a thousand men consisting of merchants and farmers, monks and ordinary serfs. About a hundred women wanted to join the procession, but this number diminished after Matwilda had weeded out the known prostitutes.

On Sunday morning, May 24, 1096, the Gretz contingent formed up outside the city gates, an orderly crowd of peasants waiting for the arrival of Gunter and his men from the north. At about ten o'clock outriders appeared, soon followed by a host of some six thousand, and it was quickly apparent that the care which Count Volkmar had given to the selection of men from Gretz had not been duplicated by Gunter when he chose the volunteers at Cologne; for he appeared with a rabble. Thieves, men sprung from jail and notorious prostitutes were conspicuous. There were gangs of debtors who had shaken free of their creditors and peasants who would hoe the fields no more. Boredom had banished and the frenzy of unknown adventure was high as Gunter, now splendid in new armor and red tunic with a blue cross, spurred his horse through the wagons and the cattle. He was attended by eleven knights, and these were not rabble but hardened young men capable of defending themselves and the unruly crowd they led.

'Did you ever see such an army?' Gunter cried with animal joy as the knights rode up to welcome the new recruits.

Volkmar made no reply, but as the mob pressed in upon his own well-disciplined people he suggested, 'Let Wemzel bless us as we start,' and all uncovered as the priest intoned, 'Dear God, protect this holy army as we march to Jerusalem to recover it from the infidel. Strengthen our arms, for we fight Your battle. Sweet Jesus, lead us, for we wear Your cross. Death to the infidel!'

The multitude echoed, 'death to the infidel!' and at this unfortunate moment a Jew of Gretz who sold clothes in the market happened to pass the gates, and Gunter cried, 'Great Jesus! Why should we ride to Jerusalem to fight His enemies there and leave His greater enemies here to prosper?'

And in the heat of the moment he dashed
with a loud cry through the gates and with one
swipe of his great sword slatted off the head
of the unsuspecting Jew. The mob howled its
approval, and men from the north started
spurring their horses into the city, followed
by thousands on foot.

'Kill the Jews!' they bellowed.

A Jewish woman was coming to market, and
a lancer ran her through, using his tremendous strength to toss her in the air, where she
hung suspended for a terrible moment, her
eyes still seeing the sudden mob beneath her.
The crowd shrieked and she descended sick-
eningly toward the street, where they
trampled her to death.

Volkmar, sensing what must follow, tried to
fight his way back into the city, but he was
powerless. 'Stop!' he begged, but none would
listen.

The mob was after Jews but could not have
explained why. In the obligatory Easter ser-
mons they had listened to, ill-informed
priests crying, 'the Jews crucified Jesus Christ
and God wants you to punish them.' From
learned discourses delivered by bishops, they
had discovered that in the Old Testament,
Isaiah himself had prophesied that a Virgin

would give birth to Jesus Christ, and that the Jews had stubbornly rejected the teaching of their own Book: 'For this sin they shall be outcast forever.' And in their daily life they watched as the Jew lent money, which honest men were forbidden to do, and some had known at firsthand the interest which moneylenders charged. But stronger than any of these complaints was the inchoate suspicion, not often expressed in words, that in a world where all decent men were Christian, there was something intolerably perverse in a group who clung obstinately to an earlier religion which had been proved in error. The Jews were a living insult to the trend of history, and if one helped exterminate them, he must be doing God's work. Therefore, when Gunter pointed out the folly of marching to Jerusalem to confront God's enemies while the greater foe stayed here in Gretz, he awakened a score of latent hatreds.

'Kill the Jews!' the mob roared, storming its way through the gates, and local residents -- who had no specific cause for cursing Jews -- were caught up in the frenzy and suddenly turned informer. 'In that house a Jew lives!' Like locusts the mob descended upon the house, killing, pillaging and laying waste.

'Get the moneylender!' cried a man who had never borrowed from any Jew, and like a monstrous animal the crowd turned with one accord and swept into the southern corner of the city, where a Christian led them to Hagarzi's four-storied house. Fortunately, the banker was absent, but soldiers flushed out his daughter, whom they ran through with two lances, throwing her far over their shoulders. As she flew in the air it became evident that she was pregnant, and women shrieked approvingly, 'With that one you caught two!' And they stamped her to pieces.

'The synagogue!' they shouted, and this low building so unlike a church infuriated them, for when they came to that holy place they found that some sixty-seven Jews had taken refuge inside. 'Burn them all!' the mob screamed, and about the entrances chairs and scraps of wood were placed, drenched with oil, and set afire. When gasping Jews tried to fight their way free they were greeted with lances jabbing them back into the flames. All perished.

They were the lucky ones, for now the Crusaders started flushing out Jewish women. Old ones they killed on the spot, running them through with daggers. Younger ones they stripped naked and raped time after time in the town square, with all applauding. Then, in disgust, they hacked off the girls' heads.

For two sickly hours the Crusaders stormed through the streeets of Gretz, killing and maiming and defiling. When at last they leaned weary on their swords, with blood on their tunics and smoke in their eyes, they justified their slaughter to each others: 'It would have been folly to leave for Jerusalem when the men who crucified our Saviour stayed behind to grow rich.' When they withdrew from the city they left behind eighteen hundred dead Jews and the beginning of a heritage that would haunt Germany forever.

For all of their thousands of years of being driven from place to place and being persecuted, the Jewish faith has not been weakened. In fact, as Will Durant, the historian, writes, "The Jews who are as old as history, may be as lasting as civilization."

CHRISTIANITY

The dogma of Christianity is based on the teachings of Jesus of Nazareth in Galilee whose birth marks the beginning of our calendar years. The word, "Christ," comes from a Greek word meaning "Messiah," or savior of the Jewish people.

Jesus of Nazareth

Born in a manger, Jesus came to the public's attention when he was twelve, but it was when he was thirty that he began his public teaching. He was baptized by John and was referred to as a Rabbi, a teacher of the Jewish religion, Judaism.

Using simple language, he spoke as God the Father and said that He was the Son of God. He spoke of the Kingdom to Come and the Kingdom within man. His twelve disciples probably saw him as the spiritual Messiah, the promised deliverer of the

Jewish people. He spoke also a new idea: he told people to LOVE THEIR ENEMIES.

Jesus's message was for people to prepare for the Kingdom to Come. One should do penance so that one might achieve salvation by ascending to heaven at death. As in other religions, possessions are an encumbrance. "Lay you not up treasures on earth...But lay up for yourselves treasures in heaven." Each man is faced with the alternative to be accepted into Heaven or to be rejected and go to Hell.

Jesus was adored. People flocked to hear him, and as his popularity grew, his enemies increased. During a Jewish holiday He was charged with a crime of blasphemy and crucified between two thieves. On the third day it was reported that His tomb was empty.

After His crucifixion, His following grew. People spoke of Him as though He were alive, referring to Him as God and Savior, one who promised salvation to mankind. Since then, the religion of Christianity has been, for most, a Trinitarianism (belief in three) based on the worship of Father (God), the Son, and the Holy Spirit. The three are equal, eternal, and indivisible. However, it is considered mostly a mystery. There are many Christian sects, though, that do not believe in the Holy Trinity.

Jesus said that He came to establish harmony between man and God that had been broken by sin, and that His own death would release mankind from evil. It was St. Paul who later said that Christ's teaching brought the perfect knowledge of God which had been lost through sin. He preached not knowledge but faith. To the believer His meaning is revealed.

In the *Bible*, Jesus is portrayed as a good, kind, moral, and unselfish divinity. However, when the movie, "The Last Temptation of Christ," was released in 1988, it pictured Jesus as sexually desirous. Many Christians were offended by this. They attempted to have the movie banned, but on the whole, were unsuccessful because First Amendment Rights to the United States Constitution prevailed.

In addition to the Trinity, Christianity offered other differences from Judaism, such as a more extensive use of baptism. Most religions have used water in sacramental cleansing rituals, but the Christian philosophy expressed the belief that baptism was the acceptance of the life of Christ and the Holy Spirit.

An exclusive Christian ritual is the Eucharist which is the ritualistic eating of bread identified with the body of Jesus, and the sacrament of drinking wine, identified with Christ's blood. The Eucharist, also known as Holy Communion, celebrates a unity with Christ and symbolically recollects the life, death, and resurrection of Christ.

The *Bible*, which consists of the Old and New Testaments is the book of Christianity. The Old Testament is of Jewish authorship and was complied about 100 A.D. The New Testament, of Christian authorship, was compiled about 400 A.D. The gospels are the life of Jesus.

The great struggle of Christianity's beginnings survived the Roman persecution. The Christians represented to their enemies a non-violent power that no physical force could destroy. Though they were tortured and tormented, they did not fight back. In fact, they "turned the other cheek," and used the weapon of loving their enemies as Jesus had taught them.

The history section of this study discusses some of the reasons for the collapse of the Roman Empire. To review one of the reasons, it was stated that any power which attempts to control (or govern) people has to have a system of rewards for good behavior and punishments for bad. At the time of the Roman Empire, whether in Rome or in Jerusalem, Christianity had a better system of rewards and punishments than the government did. Christianity offered life everlasting in Heaven: The Romans could only offer the impermanence of earthly material things, which Christianity rebuked. The Roman Empire was several hundred years in its deterioration: The Christian religion was several hundred years in its strengthening.

Around 400 A.D. Christianity had established itself as the religion of the Western world. It is very probably true that Christianity was the savior of all the learning of the Western world that has come to us from Antiquity. Without the diligence of the Christian monks in the monasteries in Ireland and elsewhere in Europe who copied and recopied the little knowledge that had survived the Barbarian invasions during and after the Fall of Rome, Western civilization would very likely have been lost to the world altogether.

Christianity had difficult competition when the Islamic religion began in 600 A.D. by Mohammed in Arabia. Islam (also known as Moslem) spread like "wildfire" through the countries on both sides of the Mediterranean through North Africa, over to Spain, France, Italy, Turkey, and Iran. But Christianity survived that too, and though the religion was born of peace and non-violence, the Christians learned to return Islamic militancy with their own.

The Crusades

During the Medieval Period, the Christians in Europe whipped up a religious fervor to save the Holy Land from the Moslems and the Turks. These long and difficult journeys were known as the Crusades. People set out as pilgrims on horseback, and on foot, to make the long walk covering thousands of miles across Europe and into the Holy Land. There they waged war on the infidel. (An infidel or a heretic is one who believes differently than the person who calls him that name.)

Thousands of people, the very poor as well as the very rich, left on the Crusades with high hopes. For many of the leaders, these hopes may have been more political than religious. But though thousands of people left on each Crusade, those returning numbered only in the hundreds, the rest having died along the way, or having been killed in battle with the infidel.

Over a period of a couple of hundred years there were ten waves of people, or ten Crusades, setting out for the Holy Land. The one most astonishing to consider is the Children's Crusade wherein thousands of leaderless children set out for Jerusalem to do their part for their Lord, but were sold into slavery in Africa before they had barely started.

Thus the Crusades had started with lofty ideals and had ended in disgrace. They accomplished nothing in the Holy Land. There were times when the Crusaders captured the Holy Land, when they built forts, but were unable to hold out against the strength of the infidels and were forced to surrender. But the Crusades did prove at least one important thing: Christianity was a powerful unifying force by 1200 A.D. Most of Europe had assembled under the banner of Christianity in a breadth of territory that would have made any conqueror envious.

Church Power

The areas of Europe in the Middle Ages were ruled politically by Feudal Lords, but it was the Christian Church and not a king or governor or any parliament which came to rule over the Lords and their subjects. The Church was the power in the Middle Ages and as any power can be good or bad or both, the Church began to abuse its power at the same time that it offered Everlasting Life after death to souls on earth who found life difficult.

Headquartered in Rome, the Church's power lay in levying taxes, and forgiving sins. What temptations there were in this combination! Had there been checks and balances within the church structure as there are, for instance, in the Constitution of the

United States which recognizes the possible abuse of power, the history of the Western world might have been quite different. But history works its own checks and balances, though it sometimes takes hundreds of years for things to "right" themselves. Power that has been abused will be suffered for just so long before it is raised to more humanitarian levels.

In Medieval Europe it had become a practice for Church leaders to forgive the sins of certain church members depending upon their ability to contribute money to the church. This practice was known as "selling indulgences," and it was highly criticized by many devout people. While this was going on, history was working one of its many levelling processes. The printing press, one of the great equalizers of all times, had been invented, with the result that more people were learning to read. Up until about 1500 almost all important works had been printed by hand and in Latin. These books were for a very limited number of upper class people who could read. Now, with the printing presses, the Bible was published in the language of the land, French, Spanish, German, Italian, and English. Ordinary people could interpret the Bible for themselves. It was an "eye-opener!"

The Rise of Protestantism

At the same time as the invention of the printing press, Martin Luther, in Northern Germany, protested certain practices that he and many others felt were not in line with the original tenets of Christianity. He wanted to reform the church by eliminating:

1. The selling of indulgences;
2. The authority of the Pope;
3. The invocation of saints;
4. The masses for the dead:
5. The compulsory confession.

The Church listened, "cleaned house," and began to discipline church officials who were reported selling indulgences. But it did not eliminate the other practices. Martin Luther had no intention, originally, of starting a new division of Christianity; he had only meant to improve the existing church. But when there were insufficient changes to make a difference, the protestors originated their own church which was known from then on as the Protestant church. Those who remained under the existing Christian church structure became known as Catholics, meaning Universal.Under the Protestant Christian religion there are many sects, differing in their interpretation of the Bible.

Eastern Christian Church

No discussion of Christianity can exclude mention of the time, before the rise of Protestantism, when the church split into Eastern and Western establishments in 1054 A.D. This split caused the creation of the Church-State known as the Byzantine

Empire with its capitol at Constantinople which is now Istanbul.

The theology between the Eastern and Western church differs in that the Eastern church does not recognize the Pope, or purgatory nor does it recognize Rome as the center of the church. The art, music, architecture of Eastern Orthodox and the Western church are also markedly different.

Conclusion

In all of the sects of Christianity there are many differences in architecture, music, art, rituals, liturgy, and intensity of worship. Christianity embraces a multitude of different variations of interpretations, all evolving around the concepts of God, Jesus Christ, and/or the Holy Spirit, and the degree to which each sect accepts these concepts either in their entirety or singly.

Differences evolve within any religion which has come down through the ages. So to say, for instances, that Hinduism is one thing and one thing only, or to say the same for Buddhism, Judaism, Islam, or Christianity would be not only untrue, but to some people blasphemous. This short review is intended to be broad enough to be true, but not so broad as to be vapid.

ISLAM

Today, one third of the nations of the world practice the Islamic religion, which is also referred to as Moslem, Muslim, Mohammedism, or Muhammedism, though the word, "Moslem," is the most used to designate the religion. The word, "Islam," means "submission to the will of Allah."

Mohammed

This religion was started about 600 A.D. by Mohammed, who was born in Mecca, Arabia. Mohammed rejected the religion of the Arabians, who worshipped about 360 gods, and he also rejected the Trinitarianism of Christianity. Among all the Arabian gods, the most important one was Alihah, who later became known as Allah.

In Mohammed's time there was a Jewish tradition about the Messiah who was to come. There had also been a history of prophets, namely, Adam,

Noah, Abraham, Moses, and Jesus. Mohammed said that he came not as a Messiah, that he had no divinity, that he was a prophet as the others had been, and that he would work no miracles. He was honored by both the Christians and the Jews as one prophet in the line of prophets.

He emphasized that he, Mohammed, was the LAST of the prophets who would ever appear, and the revelations that God made to him through his angel, Gabriel, were the LAST revelations that would ever be made.

Mohammed had been born an orphan. He worked as a shepherd and camel driver as a young man. At the age of 40 he married a woman who was financially able to support him and this gave him considerable leisure.

At first Mohammed's message about Allah was not accepted by the people. They did not want to give up their polytheism. When he started his religion, his first convert was his wife, Khadjah. Though the religion now numbers over five hundred million people, Mohammed was not a successful proselytizer in his own home town, Mecca. He moved to a distant city, Medina, and there his new religion "caught on." He had been ridiculed in Meccas, so when the Meccan trading caravans came through Medina, he and his converts attacked them.

There had always been raids on traveling caravans, but booty and honor had been the important goals. The Bedouin tribesmen often earned their honor by raiding other tribes. Now there was a new fierceness and different goals in these raids: to destroy the infidel and the persecutors of the Islamic religion, and to kill in the name of Allah.

Prior to Mohammed, baby girls were often buried alive in the desert, and women were considered mere property. Mohammed forbid this burying of baby girls and he made it mandatory that daughters get something in inheritance. Also, being an orphan himself, Mohammed was greatly concerned for the care of orphans.

Mohammed sanctified marriage and polygamy, limiting the number of wives to four. Marriage, he said, had to be equitable to all four wives. Polygamy did not originate with Mohammed. It had been an on-going practice in many Arabian tribes.

According to the Islamic religion, it is a sin for anyone to paint even an imaginary picture of Mohammed. And anyone who writes of him in a derogatory fashion is subject to terrible punishment. When the British author, Salman Rushdie, wrote his book, Satanic Verses, 1989, which portrayed Mohammed in an unflattering manner, the leader of the Islamic religion, the Ayatollah Khomeini, offered millions of dollars to anyone who would kill the author, who was described as blaspheming Mohammed.

Islam Rituals and The Koran

One day when Mohammed was spending some time meditating in a cave at Mt. Hira, three miles from Mecca, he saw the Angel Gabriel who appeared before him. The Angel Gabriel asked him to recite a message from heaven, which became the first words of the *Koran* and which are said to be the direct words of God. Mohammed claimed that over a period of twenty-two years the entire *Koran* was revealed to him in this way.

Determined to pass on God's message, Mohammed fervently sought converts to the tenets of the *Koran.* He said that Allah had sent down the *Koran* just as He had sent the *Torah* to Moses and the Gospel to Jesus. He said the *Koran* was a sequel to those revelations. Incidentally, the word, "*Torah*" comes up frequently in the *Koran.*

The *Koran*, which is the book of Islam, gives the rules for morals and manners. and being the law of God, it cannot be added to nor subtracted from. It is considered a legal document. Unlike Christianity, there are no miracles in the Islamic religion with the exception of the *Koran*, which is considered to be a Divine Message. It reflects the direct communication of God to Mohammed.

Mohammed believed that the Jews and the Christians had corrupted the revelations, but that he, Mohammed, was bringing the CLEAR revelations. The *Koran* is considered to be a heavenly book, a literal copy of the one that exists with Allah in heaven and it is not from the mind of man. Written in poetic prose style it has a subtle kind of rhythm. It is the sum and substance of Islam. It sets out one's responsibility to Allah. A person is a Moslem if he or she accepts the *Koran.* It is a law code and it sets forth the duty of the Moslem in the Five Pillars of Faith:

1. Profession of Faith- SHAHADAH: Moslems make this declaration, "There is no God but Allah and Mohammed is the prophet of Allah."

"He has no son."

"Other gods that existed before are false."

"Jews and Moslems agree on this."

2. Prayer - SADAT: Moslems pray five times a day - at dawn, noon, mid-afternoon, sunset, and night, facing, or actually bowing to Mecca. They use a rug if they are praying elsewhere than in a Mosque. The MUEZZIN summons the Moslems to prayer. He mounts a tower at appropriate hours and the people respond. The tower is a Minaret and there are usually several minarets at each Mosque, the place of worship for Moslems. There is no priesthood, no hierarchy, No notion of sacrifice or things done at an alter.

3. Fast - RAMADAN: Moslems may not eat or drink during the daylight hours of the ninth lunar month. After sunset things change back to the action of the day. It was during the ninth lunar month that Mohammed received the first message from God from the Angel Gabriel. Fasting atones for evil deeds and makes it possible to commune more intimately with God.

4. Tithe - ALMS ZAKAT; A certain percentage of each Moslem's income goes into a central coffer. This money is used to help the poor.

5. Pilgrimage - HAJJ: Most Moslems have a great desire to go on a pilgrimage to Mecca at least once in a lifetime. At Mecca the pilgrims dress all in a special seamless garment signifying that all men are equal in the eyes of Allah. They circle around the

Kaaba seven times as Mohammed did when he destroyed all Gods except Allah. Pilgrims kiss the Black Stone at the Kaaba each time they circle. In Moslem tradition the Black Stone is said to have been borne to earth by the Angel Gabriel.

Pilgrims go out to Mt. Hira where Mohammed received the first revelation from the Angel Gabriel. One who has made a pilgrimage may put the word, "Hajj" pilgrim, in front of his name. No women are permitted to make this pilgrimage.

Women are excluded from certain sections of Mosques, and women still veil their faces from men other than their family, a practice called PURDAH.

The Moslem ritual of repeating the name of Allah, as one counts one's beads, was borrowed from Hinduism. There is a certain rhythm and a certain breathing control and one is not meant to speed through this rite. Even in religious dancing, especially the Whirling Dervish, the name of Allah is constantly repeated.

The Growth of Islam

For the Moslem there is a final judgment: Paradise for the true believer and hell for the non-believer. And a Moslem who dies fighting for Allah goes to paradise instantly. Raids to acquire converts to Islam became brutal and they brought with them a new aspect of war.

JIHAD became the name describing the warring struggle against those who opposed Islam. This religion was spread by the message, but it was also

---

spread very much by the sword. "Fight in the way of God. Slay them, persecution is more grievous than slaying." Jihad was against paganism but it was not just a raid. It was a holy war and religious obligation.

Islam was not, at least in the early years, against the Christians and the Jews. It was against the pagans. The Moslems thought the Christians and Jews would join Islam because they all worshipped the one and the same God. When the Christians and Jews did not convert to Islam the Moslems began their attack on these two religious groups.

In spite of some opposition from the intellectuals who attempted to deny Mohammed's whole prophetic message, Islam spread around Arabia and the Mediterranean and into Spain. Its rapid invasion of Europe was stopped in France in the Battle of Tours in 732. Wherever Islam took hold, its followers left beautiful mosaic tiled mosques as testimony of their devotion to Allah. The Taj-Mahal in India, one of the most beautiful buildings in the world was built by a Moslem ruler after the death of his beloved wife.

Conclusion

The religion of Islam is very simple. There are no rituals, no baptism, no unattainable goals, no goals reserved only for the most devout. One simply accepts and one is a Moslem. It is possible in other religions to separate one's spiritual life from one's everyday life; not so in Islam. The Islamic religion is built into most of the day's activities as set forth in the *Koran*.

CHAPTER FOUR

A SHORT HISTORY OF ART

As with all other art forms, visual art is a comment on life at the time. So a history of art is a valuable adjunct to the history of people in a certain place on earth. As Catherine Anne Porter wrote, "The Arts outlive governments and societies that create them."

The first section of this chapter will include a short discussion on visual art. One must remember that in this short book only the main art periods through history can be brought out and those only briefly. On this subject and others, readers are encouraged to explore further. If we start with the cave drawings in France, we can make some intelligent estimates of life in prehistoric times.

CAVE ART

Far back in remote caves, especially in Spain and France, there are colorful pictures of animals painted on rock walls dating back to about 15,000 B.C. One of the richest finds of cave art was discovered by two teenage boys out rabbit hunting in Lascaux, France. Their dog dropped down into a hole enlarged by a recent storm. The boys took sticks and knives and opened the hole larger to find their dog. They slid down twenty five feet into a large chamber where they lit matches to find their way. There they discovered more rooms painted with huge animals. One fresco of bulls was seventeen feet long. There were other paintings of cows, sixty horses, stag's heads six cat-like animals, and two dark brown bison. The animals are large and realistically full of life.

The Stag Hunt
A cave painting in the Cueva de los
Caballos, Albocacer, Castellon, Spain.

Opinions vary on the purpose of this prehistoric art. One opinion says that men gathered before a hunt back in these caves to conduct a ritual on which they revered and then symbolically conquered the animals as they hoped to do the next day. Because the meat from the hunt was a good source of food for the group, success in the hunt was very important.

A later opinion says that young boys may have been initiated into their puberty rites in these remote caves by the men of the tribe. In these rituals a boy was taught that his value as a man depended on his huntsmanship, his ability to bear pain, and his ability to keep the particular secret of the ritual from others, particularly females. The drawings tell him that life is "kill or be killed." One of the stick figures in one cave drawing, depicting a man being trampled, demonstrates the vulnerability of human life when up against the large animals. Whatever the purpose of these drawings, they are still a mystery.

Though there is discrepancy of opinion as to the interpretation of cave art, there is little discrepancy of opinion as to the quality of the art. The lines of the animals are graceful, and the shading of the pigmented colors are harmoniously subtle. While the pictures of the people are simple, the pictures of the animals are developed with mature realism.

Most of the caves in which these drawings were found are now shut off from the public. It became apparent that the air conditioning which had been installed had contributed to the growth of algae which was destroying the pigment. A chemical was found to eliminate the algae without hurting the art, and tourists were kept out of the caves for a long period of time. Now only five people a day selected for study purposes, may enter and then only for thirty five minutes as a group. The reason we have such a good look at this prehistoric art is that it was sealed up for thousands of years, airtight and tomb-like. With vigilance the "birth of art" is again being carefully preserved.

EGYPTIAN ART

A great deal of the art of Ancient Egypt of about 3000 B.C. has also been sealed up, purposefully, in the tombs of the rulers. Many tombs of the god-

Tomb of Nakht, Thebes, c. 1450 B.C.

kings were later ransacked, the interior art works carried off, and the paintings on the walls left to survive the invading elements of sand and wind. But a few tombs escaped destruction and have only recently been opened. King Tut's tomb is a prime example of this. The artifacts and the paintings on the walls are as they were put there, and they enable us to make the historic leap back to his lifetime. In the various tombs we can see pictures of servants and rulers in everyday life scenes.

In addition to the tombs, there are many other good art forms to study for an understanding of ancient Egyptian art. In most of these we can see that the human figure has taken on significant importance over the prehistoric stick figures in the cave art.

In paintings, the Ancient Egyptian portrayed people in full form, though almost always in profile.

In Egyptian art, a person's eye unrealistically faces the viewer.

The stone statues of the Early Egyptian periods by later standards are not graceful. They are bulky and somewhat squat in proportion, though that may have been the physique there at that time. Compare the statues of Egypt and Greece and notice the graceful, flowing Grecian form with the bulky Egyptian form.

EGYPT

GREECE

Khafre, side and front, Gizeh. C 2600 B.C.

Polyklettos, Doryphoros, original C. 450-440 B.C.

GRECIAN ART

Looking at the Egyptian and Grecian statues you will see that the Greek lines of the body are more rounded, more soft looking than the Egyptian. Whether of gods, goddesses, or men, or women, the Greek statues are more human looking than the earlier Egyptian statues. In cave drawings, people were represented by stick figures. In Egyptian statues, people are stiff and stone-like, while in the Greek statues, people, and even gods and goddesses, are life-like, their human qualities predominating.

The civilization of Ancient Greece is said to be, to this day, unequalled, and credit for its glory is given in large part to the promotion of the arts by civic leaders. Greek dramatists and other artists were supported by the government, providing a necessary part of the pride that accompanies a successful civilization.

Let us take a look at our own country in that respect. Who is encouraging artistic creativity? Actually there is considerable support. The National Endowment for the Arts, and National Center for the Humanities and other individual and state agencies lend support and encouragement to artistic development. The results of this governmental interest cannot help but contribute to our sense of pride in the United States.

ROMAN ART

Pride is an absolute necessity for a culture's continuance. One of the many reasons given for the collapse of the Roman Empire is that, although they contributed in other ways, the Romans copied most of their art forms from the Greeks. They did not contribute any significant unique art form on which the Empire could base its pride. The one original creation from the roman Empire was the marble statue which portrayed a person from the shoulders up. This is called a "bust," and was most often a representation of an important governmental leader.

Hadrian, C. A.D. 120. Marble,
Museo Ostiense, Ostia

The Greek influence passed on to Rome and throughout the Roman Empire which spread from the Tigris Euphrates Rivers to the borders of Scotland. The great thrust of Roman energy was devoted to the conquest and administration, law and government, with less energy devoted to the arts. Greek art dominated the Roman scene. The Roman contribution to building the stone archways will be discussed in the architectural history chapter.

MEDIEVAL ART

The collapse of the Roman Empire heralded, in pathetic tones, a long period in Western Civilization which for most people was filled with misery, disease, banditry, and exploitation. If there was any hope at all it came in the shape of the Christian cross.

Otto III Enthroned Receiving the Hommage of
Four Parts of the Empire

If life were near to unbearable on earth it couldn't help but be better in the "hereafter" if one led a good Christian life. It has been said that Christianity would never have made its start if the Romans hadn't been so cruel, or if the Medieval Period hadn't held so little hope for the masses of people. Christianity offered hope.

The Annunciation to the Shepherds, 997-1000.

The art, therefore, of this period in the Western world, depicts religious scenes, or is manifest in the statues or buildings or in the music, all demonstrating devotion to the Christian religion.

Even though some artists might have been thwarted by religious leaders if they had wanted to create other than religious art, the chances would probably have been slim that they would have had other subjects uppermost in their minds at that time. The church was ALL. Look at the thrust of creativity commemorating Christianity in the Gothic Cathedrals, the paintings of the Virgin Mary, The Christ Child, and the Crucifixion.

As you observe, you will notice a certain stiffness of body and calculated balance of composition not so evident in the Renaissance period which followed the Medieval period. Whereas Christianity was the focal point of art in the Medieval period, the PERSON was the focal point of art in the Renaissance. The church power gave way to national power when individual feudal provinces merged and eventually over a long period of time evolved into nations.

RENAISSANCE ART

In the Medieval period, as was mentioned in the history section of this writing, one may not have known in what geographical section one lived, but one surely knew the bishopric or church area. Now, in the Renaissance, territorial, geographical rights had been established. These geographical areas were not so often in the name of the church, but in the name of, at first, certain strong feudal lords and then later in the name of nations as they were formed.

Emerging nations promoted exploration. One thing leads to another in no predictable order. Men travel the waters (even to America in 1492) and things like the compass become more important, if not essential. Navigation was made easier with the invention of the sextant. Previously, in order to find out how far north or south the ship was, the mariner needed something with which he could measure the angle between the horizon and the sun at noon, or some fixed star. The astrolabe was used but it was too difficult when the ship was heaving from side to side. So the cross-staff was used for many centuries until the sextant was invented, a reflecting quadrant which was an arc measuring the sixth of a circle. Sights could be taken easier without regard to the roll of the ship.

The invention of the telescope, the discovery of the law of gravity, the realization that the sun and NOT the earth is the center of the universe, the Newtonian theories of force, the invention of the printing press, the philosophical questioning of religious concepts of Martin Luther and John Calvin, all of these and more in the Renaissance, opened up new ways for people to view themselves, and this affected their perspective on art.

Christianity was and still is a powerful influence on art, but with the beginning of the Renaissance, there was this influx of other influences on human life that artists incorporated into their work. Renaissance artists put PEOPLE, not the church, as their central point of study. Even though many still were of religious subjects, the art forms of the Renaissance brought out the HUMAN quality of the subject. Look at Michelangelo's carving of "*David*,"

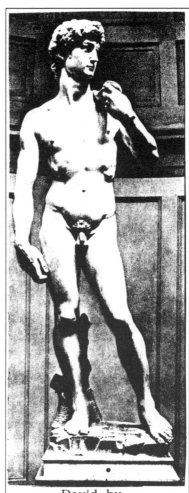

David, by
Michelangelo.
1501

and compare it with some works of the Medieval period.

Look, too, at the non-religious portraits and pictures of other Renaissance artists and see how easy it is to put yourself into the emotion of the people.

Human beings had come a long way in importance to themselves as portrayed by artists since the prehistoric cave art. Freed, then, from the bonds of church prescription of what artists MUST do, artists accepted the patronage (support) of people newly rich from the crusader's trading. Artists were supported by Popes and also by businessmen to do whatever work individually pleased the patron. First in Florence, Italy, and then in Holland, artists explored their new freedom to paint non-religious subjects. Out of their period we have the heritage of the great masters, Michelangelo, Leonardo da Vinci, Bruegel the Elder, Titian, Cellini, Rubens, and others.

Leonardo da Vinci,
Youth With a Lance, c. 1513

MODERN ART

Naturalism

Artists began to transfer their skills from portraying the HUMAN CONDITION as a subject, to portraying the REALISM OF NATURE. Certain artists in this "naturalist" period, namely Watteau, David, Goya, Constable, Gainsborough, Delacroix, painted either the horrendous confrontation with

Eugene Delacroix
The massacre at Chios, 1822-24.

violence or the romantic view of natural landscapes, full and generous with trees, rivulets, and clouds.

This "naturalist" period is almost simultaneous with the period in music known as the Romantic period. This was the time of sentimental, emotional, harmonious melodies of Beethoven, Schubert, Chopin, and Brahms, to name a few. These pictorial and musical art forms evolved at the same time as the philosophical discussions about the importance of the common man. Philosophically this was the Age of Enlightenment which produced such men as John Locke, Montesqueiu, Voltaire, and Rousseau. Out of this questioning of the rights of common people, the French Revolution erupted.

Impressionism

While old philosophical arguments persist, artists seek a different reality in their search for the meaning of life. Art is a comment on life at the time, and is often a reaction to the period of art which preceded it. Rejecting realism and naturalism, artists turned toward what became known as IMPRES-SIONISM.

After the camera was invented, around 1850, it was felt that there was little point in painting a picture of something that could be more accurately captured in a photograph. The new artists of the late 1880's and 1900's said, art should NOT be an exact duplication of a subject, but it should be the artists' impression of the subject. And so IMPRESSIONIS-

TIC art was developed. It was a birth with a difficult struggle, as are all new art forms.

When Cezanne, Van Gogh, Gauguin, and others first exhibited their "distorted" pictures as they were called, the public was repulsed. Now their paintings today are priceless. They showed people a

Van Gogh -
Self Portrait, 1887

new way to look at things. And why not? The world was changing, so art, which reflects or comments on life, must also necessarily change.

Impressionistic pictures were meant to show,

Cezanne -
Still Life with Apples, 1879 - 1882

not the way a person actually looked, or the way a wheat field looked, but its attempt was to picture the emotionalism of the moment, but not realistically as the Renaissance painters had done. The impressionists introduced a fresh look at things we had taken for granted. Still-life picture of the impressionistic period have a certain brusqueness: they are not the velvet smooth renditions of previous art periods.

The portraits of the impressionistic period reveal a different picture of a person than would have been painted by, for instance, Renaissance painters.

The music of the period did the same thing. It gave an emotional IMPRESSION of something. Debussy's "*The Sea*" and Stravinsky's "*The Rites of*

Edvard Munch, The Scream, 1893.
Nasjonalgalleriet, Oslo.

Spring," are more concerned with an impression of the subject than in providing an expected melody to carry the listener along. Impressionism requires some effort on the part of the viewer or listener. Impressionistic painters and musicians deserted the expected. This was difficult for audiences to accept.

Abstraction

Artists did not stop with Impressionism. They have gone on to Abstraction, into Design Art, into Super-Realism. The abstraction carries with it the essence of an idea, which is not as clearly portrayed as it would be in Impressionism. If the Impressionists

Pablo Picasso, Guernica, mural, 1937.

confounded the viewers, just think what the Abstractionists did! There were at least recognizable people, landscapes, or things in an Impressionistic painting, but very little if any realism in abstract art

The main idea of abstract art is that the viewers should put themselves into the interpretation of the picture. As in any art, if the emotion of the "spectator," is similar to the emotion of the creator, the art has made its point. A poet, for instance, should come close to evoking the same emotion in the reader as the poet felt in its writing.

Abstract Expressionism

Abstract art is not meant to portray SOME-THING, and this tends to disappoint spectators who

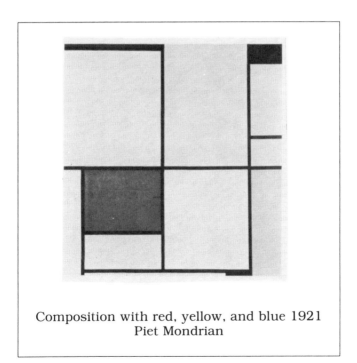

Composition with red, yellow, and blue 1921
Piet Mondrian

want their work done for them. Many people want to admire a painting on the basis of how REAL it looks. Artists today feel that how real something is portrayed may be the worst criticism. for a camera could do the same or better in an instant.

These post impressionists, Mondrian, Klee, Duchamp, Chagall, Miro, Pollock, Lichtenstein, and others could compare their paintings with the music of Charles Ives, John Cage, Stockhausen. These two current forms of art and music are related to existen-

Jackson Pollock -
Number 6, 1949

tialist philosophy, and from the literature of this period. All of these make serious consideration of CHANCE happenings, and a person's isolation.

Modern art, whether literary, pictorial, sculpture, or music, is not comforting, as for instance, Renaissance art, Romantic music, or even Impressionistic art. Today's art leaves a person to decide for themselves with what the existentialists would call the "awful responsibility of choice." Most people don't want that responsibility

Pop Art

Pop Art was a name given to artists who gave a critical look at our materialistic society. Andy Warhol's *"Four Campbell's Soup Cans, 1962"* exemplifies this art. Artists were telling us to take a close look at our values.

Op Art

Then Op (for optical) art gave us a respite from criticism, letting lines and color and non-realistic designs play on our optical nerves.

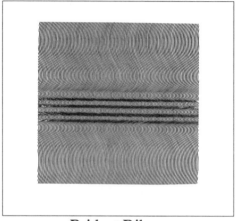

Bridget Riley -
Current, 1964

Super Realism

The art world is currently in, or very likely now leaving a period called Super-Realism, wherein artists tend to portray people, places, and things more starkly than the camera can, if that is possible. In the short period immediately preceding this, viewers were briefly freed from looking at their society and at themselves. In Op Art they had only to look at lines and color and spaces and have a visual-sensual experience. Now the Super-Realists have jerked us back to reality. They are poking fun at reality and materialism and asking us to criticize ourselves.

Below is a section of Alfred Leslie's Super-realistic self-portrait. One shouldn't generalize about a whole period from one picture, but taking just this one, what does it say to you about today? And how is it related to the search for the meaning of life?

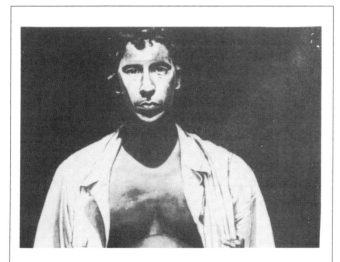

New York Whitney Museum of
American Art, 1967

Postmodernism

This is a name given to the current period in pictorial art and it includes examples of abstract and realistic art. As yet no clear-cut style seems to have emerged. It will be interesting to watch the development of various artists during the next few years.

A FEW ARTISTS THROUGH THE AGES

MEDIEVAL 400 - 1400

Renier of Huy (12th Century)
Nicholas of Verdun (12th Century)
Nicola Pisano (1258-1278)
Giovanni Pisano (c. 1245-1314)
Giotto di Bondone (c. 1266 -c. 1337)
Lorenzetti Brothers (c. 1280 -1348)
Hubert van Eyck (c. 1370-1426)
Robert Campin (1375-1444)
Filippo Brunelleschi (1377-1446)
Lorenzo Ghiberti (c. 1381-1455)
Donatello (c. 1386-1466)
Jan van Eyck (c. 1390-1441)

RENAISSANCE 1400 - 1700

Masaccio (1401-1474)
Leone Battista Alberti (c. 1401-1472)
Antonio Rossellino (1427-1479)
Giovanni Bellini (c. 1430-1470)
Sandro Botticelli (c. 1440-1510)
Leonardo da Vinci (1452-1519)
Jerome Bosch (c. 1460-1516)
Hans Holbein the Younger (1460-1524)
Albrecht Durer (1471-1528)
Michelangelo Buonarroti (1475-1564)
Raphael Sanzion (1483-1520)
Titian (1489-1576)
Correggio (1494-1534)

Benvenuto Cellini (1500-1571)
Pieter Bruegel the Elder (c. 1528-1569)
El Greco (1540-1614)
Peter Paul Rubens (1577-1640)
Diego Velazquez (1599-1660)
Rembrandt (1606-1675)
Lavinia Fontana of Bologna (1552-1614)
Artemisia Gentileschi (1593-1652)
Catharina van Hemeindesen (1528-1587)
Leonia Teerling (1515-1576)

MODERN PERIOD 1700 TO THE PRESENT

NATURALISTS
Antoine Watteau (1684-1721)
Thomas Gainsborough (1727-1788)
John Singleton Copley (1738-1815)
Louis David Jacques (1748-1825)
John Constable (1776-1837)
Eugene Delacroix (1798-1863)
IMPRESSIONISTS
Joseph Turner (1775-1851)
Edourd Manet (1832 - 1883)
James Whistler (1834-1903)
Edgar Degas (1834-1917)
Winslow Homer (1836-1910)
Paul Cezanne (1839-1906)
Claude Monet (1848-1926)
Auguste Renoir (1841-1919)
Paul Gauguin (1848-1903)
Vincent van Gogh (1853-1890)
George Seurat (1859-1891)
Henri Toulouse-Latrec (1864-1901)

REALISTS AND SUPER REALISTS
>   Andrew Wyeth 1917-
>   Roy Lichtenstein 1923-
>   Robert Indiana 1928-
ABSTRACTIONISTS
>   Henri Matisse (1869-1954)
>   Paul Klee (1879-1940)
>   Pablo Picasso (1881-1973)
>   Georges Braque (1882-1963)
>   Marc Chagall (1889-1985)
>   Joan Miro (1893-1983)
>   Georgia O'Keefe (1887-1988)
>   Salvador Dali (1904-1989)
>   Diego Rivera (1886-1957)

CHAPTER FIVE

A SHORT HISTORY OF MUSIC

Music is said to be the most powerful art and the most perishable. Its rhythm and movements of sound can arouse patriotic fervor to the point of sending men into battle. It can transform a person's mood from hostility to serenity, or vice versa. Or a simple melody can evoke memories of old friends, other places, or old love affairs. But powerful as it is, compared to architecture, sculpture, literature, or painting, music is perishable.

Unlike the other humanities, it has another quality, that of being inescapable, except to the deaf. A person can walk into a building without being aware of its architectural design. One can also walk into a room where pictures hang on the wall and hardly be conscious of their existence. But it is virtually impossible to be anywhere where music is being played and ignore it. Music affects the nerves in a way that other arts do not.

Because of its emotional appeal, music has probably always been a part of human existence. Simple instruments from prehistoric times and from antiquity have been unearthed in burial grounds and tombs. It is believed that when people joined into tribes that the important events of the group were communicated and kept alive in people's memory by verse form. Rhyming men or women were called Bards and they were in a sense the historians of the group. The rhyme and rhythm of the verses which they taught were repeated over and over again in a singing manner for easy memorization. This kind of musical history was passed from generation to generation without being written down.

MUSIC OF ANTIQUITY

The further back in musical history we go, the less we know about it . We can only guess how the music from Antiquity must have sounded. We have some knowledge of ancient instruments from fragments that have been found, and from pictures on vases, or temple walls, but musical notation was not used much until after the Golden Age of Greece, that is, not until after about 500 B.C.

Yet, even though there was practically no notation, music was very important to the ancient Greeks. Plato wrote that of all the subjects a student should study, he would consider music to be the most important because, as he said, "it tunes the soul correctly. Music was as important to the education of a young man in ancient Greece, as the three R's are to all students today. (Girls were not educated in ancient Greece). But we must remember, when we speak of music, music means different things to different people. We would have difficulty, for instance, equating the music of India with modern American Rock music.

The Greek philosopher and mathematician, Pythagoras, who lived about 450 B.C., related music to mathematics as he discovered that the strings on certain musical instruments produced different sounds depending on their length and their tautness, all of which he set up on a numbering system. His tying music with mathematics persists today, as all bars in musical notation are composed having the same number count.

A few fragments of musical notation from ancient Greece exist today and were decoded only 300 years ago. Of these fragments it is evident that the voice is more important than any instruments. Though the voice was accompanied by the kithara or the lyre, the instruments had no independent parts. The Greeks never developed music with more than one part.which is known as polyphony or harmony-Iharmony, "poly" meaning "many".)

It is the ancient Greeks who gave the Western world the present day music scale, known as the diatonic scale which we could equate with the white notes on the piano of C.D.E.F.G.A.B. This scale is so different from the musical notations of the Japanese, for instance, who have a different continuum of pitch. As Joseph Kerman writes in *A History of Art and Music*, "So in a very basic sense the language of Western music can be said to be Greek."

MEDIEVAL MUSIC

The people of the Medieval Period thought of music on three levels: heavenly, human, and instrumental, with the latter the least important. The early Christian church leaders knew the power of vocal music in persuading people to accept the faith and to worship. Instrumental music was equated with sacrificial and pagan rituals. and with dancing. Also, as the Bards of Antiquity knew, "sounded," words, or psalms and hymns which were sung repetitiously were easy to learn and to remember. Few people could read then, but they could listen and repeat words associated with melodies. And singing helped to keep the congregation awake.

Christianity and music have been linked closely since the end of Antiquity. But when the Roman Emperor, Constantine, moved the capital of his empire to what was then Constantinople, this changed not only the course of art, but also the course of music. Byzantium (the early name for Constantinople which is now Istanbul) art and music are far different from Western art and music. The Byzantine church, known as the Eastern Orothodox church, would not permit instruments, but the

Western church permitted organs in churches from early in the Medieval Period.

The one person who most significantly influenced Medieval music was St. Gregory the Great IGregory the Great (Pope from 590-604). He collected and codified the Roman Chant often referred to as the Gregorian Chant, which is one note sung without instrument or harmony and with an almost imperceptible melody.

Whereas Christian church services relied on vocal music, their monasteries relied on this music even more. Most of the days' activities were accompanied by specific chants. All Masses required specific music and as the days and months changed, so did the selection of music for the specific day or month.

The "plainsong," another word for the Chant, was declared by Emperor Chalemagne in 800 as the official church music for the Holy Roman Empire. This repertory (collection) of music is the Catholic Church music used today.

The Christian church gave inspiration to the art forms of the Medieval period, and the church also dominated the subject matter and the style of art. It was only when the church's power gave way to the power of nations as they emerged, that the artists dared to write or paint, or sing of ideas which were not religious. Courtly love was a topic that lyricists (song writers) and instrumentalists enjoyed.

RENAISSANCE MUSIC

Laced with a poignant though unrealistic sadness, or capricious, light-hearted sentiment of love, music of the Renaissance made the the human being, and *not the Church*, the subject of its message.especially in the songs sung by the troubadors. These Troubador Love Songs, or songs of Courtly love, known as chansons, of the late Medieval and early Renaissance years were the forerunners of love poetry of later years.

With the ending of the Medieval Period music gradually became more complex. Polyphony was introduced and words and music were considered in unity. As this was a period of considerable poetic writing, much of this poetry was put to music. During this time the Virgin Mary was the object of great worship and as such she received the adoration of musicians in their dedication of motets to her name, which were called *Marian motets*. Motets are choral works on a sacred text usually without instruments and with several voices.

Except for the chansons and motets, new music styles were slow to appear in the early Renaissance. The amazing new energetic forces of the Renaissance brought out new paintings, scientific discoveries, explorations, but very little of anything new in music. The music of the Medieval period was also the music of the Renaissance, that is, up to about 1600, when musicians elaborated on harmonic scales, developed new instruments, and composed an art form known as Baroque. Comparable to the architectural style of the same name, Baroque music was a welcome relief from the somber sounds of the Gregorian Chant and swooning love strains of the Troubador love songs.

Baroque music, as Baroque architecture, is involved and complicated. It has been described as "frilly," and "overdone," because it is busy, but mostly because it contrasts with the "serious" music which preceded it and followed it. In this case the word "serious" refers to the religious subject matter of the Gregorian chants in the Medieval period, and the "story line," dramatic and sometimes overly sentimental music of the Romantic period which followed the Baroque period. Some of the most famous Baroque composers were Bach, Haydn, Handel, and Mozart.

In the Romantic Era there are many composers whose names are probably quite familiar to you. If you learn the names of the Baroque musicians, Bach, Haydn, Handel, and Mozart, then you can be reasonably sure that all of the other names of famous composers, other than these four, were composers of the Romantic period. (Actually Mozart is considered a "bridge" between Baroque and Romantic in a short period referred to as "classical," but he is often referred to as a composer of the Baroque period also.)

Here are names you have probably heard before and all belong to the Romantic period: Beethoven, Chopin, Liszt, Schumann, Schubert, Brahms, Mendelssohn, Verdi, Tchaikovsky, Wagner. The music of their period has the quality of expectation about it. If a musician stopped playing in the middle of a musical phrase, chances are the listener might be able to hum the ending of the phrase, never having heard it before.

In Romantic period music there is a repetitious build-up in which the listener finds himself caught up and carried along. Music of the Romantic period does not require the listener to work at understanding the music to the degree that Baroque does, or for that matter, any music since its time. It is likely that the lack of listener concentration required is what makes Romantic period music as popular as it is.

Minnesingers and Madrigals

Other musical creations should be mentioned here. The Troubador singers had their counterpart in Germany, but under the name of Minnesingers. These latter musicians, however, were more serious than the Troubadors, emphasizing religious and church music. Out of these musical forms the madrigal evolved, important because it emphasized words more than accompaniment. Musicians often improvised as the lyrics were sung. In a sense, the madrigal was a necessary forerunner to the opera, where words are vital.

Opera

Opera which is a stage drama set to music had its beginning with Monteverdi in 1607. "Opera" is an Italian word meaning "a work. It is comparatively expensive entertainment which combines the dramatic techniques of stage setting, drama, costuming, choreography, and of course, music.

At first, operas were performed as court entertainment, often in celebration of an important person's wedding or birthday. As an entertainment style it became the rage, not only with royalty and the upper class, but also with the middle class. Venice, Italy, which had a population of 140,000, had seven opera houses in the early Renaissance years. This is about the same number for movie houses today for a city with the same population.

Like movies, operas depend on stars, have elaborate equipment for moving staging hurriedly, and large supporting casts. The star of the opera is known as a virtuoso. He or she sings Arias, which are long, sustained, and often passionate vocals, often becoming the focal point of an opera.

Opera in Venice was the most popular theater form. The wealthy bought boxes (special reserved seating sections) at the opera house and bequeathed them to their heirs. Though opera originated in Italy, it was later performed in Germany, though Italian words were used. Italian singers, composers, conductors, and directors were transported from Italy.

In Vienna, Austria, opera became popular also and Italians performed there as well. The composer, Monteverdi, was appointed as artistic director to the imperial court. The Austrian composer, Wolfgang Amadeus Mozart (1756-1791) produced his greatest works in Vienna. With his great gift for melody he composed areas which were, if not better than the Italian's, at least equal. When he wrote his first opera in German, the public was not ready to accept opera that was not Italian.

The greatest Italian composer of operas is Guiseppe Verdi (1831-1901) who began composing in his twenties and produced many of the most famous operas, including Rigoletto, Aida, Il Trovatore, until his last opera, Falstaff, composed when he was 80 years old. *Falstaff* was acclaimed a masterpiece.

MODERN MUSIC

Impressionistic Music

Music of the impressionistic composers, composed their words around 1900, Notably in the music of Debussey and Stravinsky, audiences take part in determining what's going on. Debussey is considered transitional, leading the way from traditional Romantic into the Modern period.

The music of Debussey's "*La Mer*," or translated, "*The Sea*," gives the impression of the rise and swell of the sea. Stravinsky's "*Rites* (*Rituals*) *of Spring*," endeavors to get the listener involved in impressions of a landscape awakening to spring.

Existentialism in Music

There are other musicians who followed these impressionists in the early 1900's. Charles Ives and later John Cage introduced an existentialist element into music. Things actually happened by chance in the musical score. There are few melodies in this music and what melodies there are, are apt to stop instantly, destroying the listener's expectations. Unlike Romantic, or even the impressionistic music, modern music does not make melody its most important element.

John Cage was honored by Harvard University, March, 1989, for his contribution to modern music. He has shaken people out of their conventional expectations of what music should be, composing since he was 18, always with a fresh approach to sound. Typically existentialist, Cage 76 years old in 1989, says he discovered his intention in life forty years ago and that it is "the exploration of the non-intention."

Jazz

Jazz is an Afro-American music which had its American beginnings in New Orleans probably around 1900. It is not a music which is transferred to paper because its uniqueness is in its improvisation. Jazz musicians rely on their rhythmic sense and the fundamental beat of the music. There is a group spirit within a jazz orchestra which allows for spontaneous instrumental solos -- an-on-the-spot performance with each musician taking his or her turn as lead musician. Some of the most famous jazz musicians include Louis Armstrong, Charlie Parker, and Ornette Coleman.

Rock 'n Roll

Rock music, which began in the 1950's and 1960's is currently the most popular form of music and is a great money maker. the term "rock" often referred to as rock'n'roll may have been based on a song, "Good Rockin' Tonight," or other songs whose titles had the word, "rock." Young people especially relate to this music, usually performed by young musicians who use electric guitars as the primary instrument. Often other electronic equipment is used including synthesizers and many amplifiers carrying music to huge audiences.

The first important rock soloist was Elvis Presley followed by others such as the Kingston Trio, and Bob Dylan whose songs were concerned in the 1960's with social and political issues such as civil rights, drugs, sex, and the Vietnam War. The Beatles, an English group, gained worldwide fame with their humorous and sensitive songs.

In the 1970's musicians attempted to break away from the traditional rock music, referring to their style as punk rock. While it was not commercially successful it did demonstrate that young musicians could express themselves musically without expensive equipment.

In the 1970's and 1980's rock video added another dimension to the popular music style with elaborate stage designs, acting, and dancing. Through rock video Michael Jackson became the most popular musician in the history of rock music. Other famous musicians or groups of this period include Joan Baez, Janis Joplin, Chuck Berry, Blues, Jimi Hendrix, Buddy Holly, Jazz, Led Zeppelin, AC/DC, Kiss, Allman Brothers, Rolling Stones, Paul Simon, Bruce Springsteen, The Who, Stevie Wonder, and more.

Conclusion

Can you imagine what the reaction might have been when jazz first appeared, or when the Beatles first appeared? These now seem rather old fashioned, but at one time they were shocking to hear because ears were tuned to hear old sweet melodies.

The music that young people play today, that often annoys their parents, will in turn be considered old fashioned when the next generation determines its own preference. These new choices tell the world that a new generation is alive and well. If children always selected what their parents selected, we would be no further along culturally than prehistoric people. Maybe that would be all right, but that's another subject.

In the field of music, each young generation has an ability to affect the older generation. The jazz age disturbed the elders; when Elvis Presley was young he shocked T.V. censors; the whole drug culture has at times been blamed on the Beatles who were said to have led the young astray.

Whatever musical style is in vogue now is no doubt worrying people over forty years of age, especially if they have teenage children.

"Turn it down," has been the demand of each of the past three generations, as parents shout over the noise of radios, records, or cassettes. Unlike the other arts, music is difficult to ignore, and especially so if it is loud.

Why is there such an emphasis today on volume? Could it be that the young are insisting with a loudness unequalled before that they be heard, even if it takes six sets of amplifiers? Could it be they don't believe their parents are listening to them in other ways?

Musically, electronic synthesizers create artificial sound, and computers create robots and artificial intelligence. One might compare the Renaissance search for meaning which emphasized the human being, with our search for meaning DE-EMPHASIZING the human being as we rely on computers and synthesizers. What do our creations tell us about our values at this time?

A FEW MUSICIANS AND COMPOSERS

THROUGH THE AGES

RENAISSANCE c. 1400-1700

Guillaume Duray (c.1400-1474)
Jakob Obrecht (c. 1430-1505)
Jasquin Desprez (c. 1440-1521)
Vittoria Alcotti
Francesca Baglioncella
Barbara Strozzi
Claudio Monteverdi (1567-1643)
Antonio Stradivari (1644-1737)
Antonio Vivaldi (c.1675-1741)

BAROQUE ERA c. 1600 -1750

Johann Sebastian Bach (1685-1750)
Wolfgang Amadeus Mozart (1757-1791)
    ("Bridges" Baroque and Romantic in short
    period known as "classical")
Franz Joseph Haydn (1732-1809)
George Frederic Handel (1685-1759)

ROMANTIC ERA c. 1750 - 1900

Franz Schubert (1797-1828)
Ludwig van Beethoven (1770-1827)
Giacomo Rossini (1792-1868)
Felix Mendelssohn (1809-1847)

Frederic Chopin (1810-1849)
Robert Schumann (1810-1856)
Franz Liszt (1811-1886)
Richard Wagner (1813-1883)
Guiseppe Verdi (1813-1901)
Johannes Brahms (1833-1897)
Peter Tchaikovsky (1840-1893)
Giacomo Puccini (1858-1924)

MODERN 1900 TO THE PRESENT

Antonin Dvorak (1841-1904)
Edvard Grieg (1843-1907)
Nicolai Rimsey-Korsakov (1844-1908)
Gustav Mahler (1860-1911_
Richard Strauss (1864-1949)
Jean Sebelius (1865-1957)
Sergei Rachmaninoff (1873-1943)
Arnold Schoenberg (1874-1951)
Bela Bartok (1881-1945)
Igor Stravinsky (1882-1971)
Paul Hindemith (1895-1963)
John Cage (1912-)
Charles Ives (1874-1954)
Karlheinz Stockhausen (1928-)

CHAPTER SIX

A SHORT HISTORY OF ARCHITECTURE

Architecture, too, reflects the period of history, how people lived, and what was important to them in their lives when the buildings were erected. Unlike other art forms, though, architecture is more durable. That was generally its purpose -- to extend the meaning of life of one historical period into the future. Extending one's self into the future is believed to be a way of not dying. As Brendan Gill writes in his biography of the famous architect, Frank Lloyd Wright, "Throughout history the need to outwit death has been through construction."

Why is it we find no examples of architecture in the prehistoric period? It is believed that there were not any significant buildings constructed as long as people existed in nomadic groups, traveling from place to place in search of food supplies. If shelter was erected it was left to disintegrate in the elements when the inhabitants moved on. True, civilization, it is said, cannot exist until buildings for lasting duration are built.

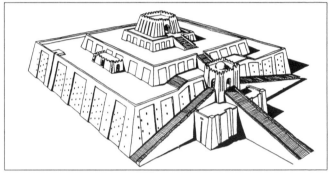

Ziggurat

As the city of Ur in Sumer is considered the birth place of civilization, we look first at the drawings of how we presume a reconstruction of the building might look. Above is a picture of the ZIGGURAT at Ur, a place of worship. Religion was a strong force which gave meaning to the lives of the people in this early city-state in about 2500 B.C. Some of the remains of this temple-like structure still stand today.

EGYPTIAN ARCHITECTURE

Many buildings from Antiquity are still standing. So careful is Egypt to ensure that its ancient architectural pyramids remain standing, that the country is embarking on a plan to preserve the Pyramids of Giza, which were built about four thousand years ago by the pharaohs Cheops,

Court and Pylon of Rameses II (c.1260 B.C.), and Colannade and Court of Amenhotep III (C. 1390 B.C.) Temple of Amen-Mut-Khonsu, Luxor

Chephren and Myncerius. The project, with expected finish date in 1989, includes a stone wall to be built around the Giza Plateau, ten miles southwest of Cairo. Foreigners will be allowed in the areas through gates. No cars will be allowed near the ancient tombs, and tour buses, will be barred from the area.

As with the ancient Egyptian pyramids, most Egyptian architecture was religiously oriented, either as temples, or tombs, or pyramids. Because the pharaohs of Egypt were considered god-kings, their tombs deify (make god-like) their persons. The early Egyptian structures were straight line and except for the triangle pyramids, they were box shaped.

GRECIAN ARCHITECTURE

The Grecians introduced a new line to their buildings. Instead of having their roofs go straight across, they built them significantly higher in the center, giving them a pitch, pointing upwards.

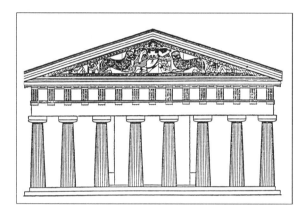

And no mention of Greek architecture should be made without pointing out the famous columns, known as Ionic, Doric, and Corinthian, named for the areas where they were built.

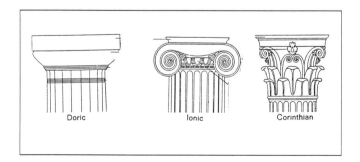

Doric   Ionic   Corinthian

ROMAN ARCHITECTURE

The Romans who contributed little to the history of art, as they were notorious copiers of Greek art, did add their dimension, however, to architecture. In an effort to get the buildings to rise further off the ground, they built an arch. Piling stone upon stone in two columns, they leaned the top stones closer to each other until there was room for one stone at the center which, by the nature of its design, would not give way to gravity pull.

The center stone in the Roman arch is known as the "keystone." Its sides slant out at the top, leaning on and securing the stones on either side. Once this arch was built, then a succession of arches could be joined together to make a dome.

Roman architecture, therefore, was much more colossal than Greek, and the domed cathedrals and government buildings have been copied down to this century. The San Francisco City Hall is a fine example of Roman architecture, dome and all. The dome, incidentally, suffered slight structural damage in the October, 1989 earthquake.

Roman architecture of Antiquity, reflecting

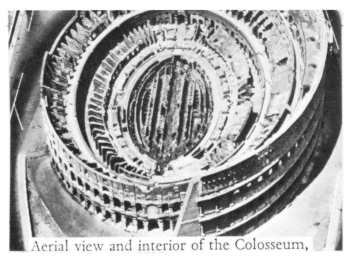

Aerial view and interior of the Colosseum, Rome, A.D. 70–82.

the time of Empire-building, epitomized governmental rather than religious influence. Palaces for emperors, senate forums, and the Coliseum for games all tell us what gave life its meaning, at least to those who were in power.

MEDIEVAL ARCHITECTURE

In the early years of the Medieval period, there wasn't much building in Western civilization. People had all they could do to survive barbarian raids, and starvation. As the years wore on, feudalism offered some sanctuary. If people know that they're going to be around for awhile they usually start building for the future. One of the requisites for civilization is that people have a sense of permanence in one place. In the mid-Medieval period, people began to dig in, in various places, principally near monasteries or church bishoprics. Remember, the Medieval period was heavily overlaid with religion. When life was dismal, people put their hopes in a future life - life after death - which Christianity offered to them in exchange for their devotion to Christ. To them, the church offered meaning.

The enormous cathedrals that were built by the devout were at first built on the old architectural lines of the Roman buildings with the Roman arch, and as such were called Romanesque. The interior floor space was interrupted with many cumbersome stone columns which were needed to hold up the connecting arches that made the ceiling.

Around the year 1100 a new device was introduced as a means of holding up the high ceilings WITHOUT the necessity of the columns in the middle of the floor.

This new creation was called a "flying buttress." It was constructed in such a way as to give support to the roof from OUTSIDE the buildings on both sides. After all, if walls that supported the roof could be reinforced so that they could hold the

Nave of Salisbury Cathedral.

weight of the roof, then the walls and roofs could reach to the sky. And that was exactly the idea! Christians saw the building of these cathedrals as a way to feel closer to God in Heaven.

This is a typical "flying buttress," the main body of the cathedral being on this side of the buttress. There would of course be another buttress on the other side of the church, giving equal support.

The foundation would be deep, to give great strength so that vaulted ceilings could extend far upward.

When the new cathedrals were being built by Germans and Frenchmen, it was said by the Italians, who believed that their Romanesque style was superior, that the new cathedrals were built by barbarians. Indeed, the Germans and the French HAD been the barbarians who had invaded Rome

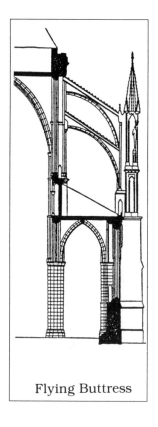

Flying Buttress

many hundred years before. One of the tribes of barbarians was the Goths. It is for this reason that the cathedrals were called Gothic.

St. Elizabeth, Marburg, 1233–83.

RENAISSANCE ARCHITECTURE

Renaissance architecture ignored the flying buttresses of the Medieval period. Both the art and the architecture of the Renaissance looked back to Antiquity to find its art forms. People looked back

Tempietto.   *c.* 1502–03. Rome.

especially to the philosophy of the Greeks, namely Socrates, Plato, and Aristotle, and back to classical architecture of the Greek and Roman periods. The architectural style of the Renaissance combined the Roman arch, the Roman dome, and the column which came down through history from the Egyptians and the Greeks. Architects made these classical features important again in the governmental and religious buildings of Italy. This style is referred to as neo-classical, meaning "new" classical.

Baroque Style

After the somewhat austere, classical period of Renaissance architecture, two other styles followed in succession. One was called Baroque, and

Royal Chapel of the palace at Versailles, 1698–1710.

the other style was termed Rococo. In music, the Baroque style gave audiences a listening challenge.

Sometimes in musical scores, with so much going on, it was hard to find the melody or its repetition or variation. This was similar in Baroque architecture too. Many frills and curls were added to the buildings. The straight-lined simplicity of Antiquity which Renaissance architects used, was abandoned in the Baroque period. This "over-done" style as it is referred to, was elaborated even more in the next architectural style which became known as Rococo.

Rococo Style

Rococo was initially a style of interior design which later appeared in exteriors. It developed after the death of France's Louis XIV almost as a reaction declaring that, since his death, things would be happier for the people of France. Rococo sculpture, painting, and architecture seem to set the stage for a party. The rooms, with their gilded moldings, and daintily colored ornament of flowers and garlands, projects a feminine appearance, not surprising since this style developed at a time when women were in prominence, holding court more or less in their homes with the intellectuals of the period. Women held the highest places in Europe -- Madame de Pompadour in France, Maria Theresa in Austria, Elizabeth in England, and Catherine in Russia.

Though Rococo started in Paris, it quickly became an international style, spreading to Austria and then to Germany, where one of the most notable buildings of this style exists. This is the Pilgrimage

church of Vierzehnheiligen (Fourteen Saints) built
by Neumann who lived from 1687-1753.

Rococo Pilgrimage church of Vierzehnheiligen
Near Bamberge, 1743-72

The interior design practically eliminates straight lines, and the ceiling decorations are bright and cheerful and receive the full play of daylight because of the large windows.

Interior Vierzehnheiligen

MODERN ARCHITECTURE

The Modern period in architecture dates from about 1900. Many styles have covered the landscapes of cities and towns throughout Europe and America. But it is the straight lines of Greek civilization and the dome of the Roman civilization that, up until recently, have been the dominant styles for governmental buildings in the Western world.

New trends are leading us in several different directions, but no one style has yet prevailed for this modern historical period. It would be difficult to determine how we will be judged by the architecture we have built. We can look back, for instance, to the architecture of the pyramids and know that they represented a culture wherein people would spend a lifetime on earth to prepare for a life after death.

How would the message in the structure of the pyramids differ from the message of the Gothic cathedrals of the Medieval period? Both the Egyptians and the Christians believed in life after death. Observe, from just these two examples how the cultural philosophy of people can be read from its buildings as well as from its writings and its art. How will future societies read our culture in THIS period?

Keep in mind that it is difficult to be analytical about an historical period while you're living in the period. That doesn't mean that we shouldn't try to determine what we are. We should. But it does mean that it is difficult to have an objective opinion because we have a biased perspective.

We are involved in today's culture. We have emotions, commitments, hopes, and despairs that necessarily color our statements. Who, then CAN be an impartial judge of our time? If not the people alive today, then the judgment for our time will fall on the generations yet to be born. They will look and see the thousands of square miles, especially in the United States, of housing tracts and will make their own analysis. These buildings with indoor plumbing and the many conveniences that would have been luxuries in any preceding historical period, will be classified and we will be labeled by future generations.

Seagram Building
New York, 1956-58.

Any analysis of the modern period will also have to take into consideration the skyscrapers, usually built for business enterprises. These new buildings reach higher than any Gothic cathedral, and they tower over their neighboring factory or residential buildings in most of the large cities of the Western world. What will all of these buildings of our time say to future generations?

COMMENTS

Judgment is difficult to make from the perspective of our own time, but future generations will interpret from our art forms what we feel now about our lives.

Guggenheim Museum, New York, 1943-59

No matter what other changes have taken place in the world since the pyramids, or since the Greek temples, or the Roman arch, or the Gothic cathedrals, there are some things which haven't changed. One of these unchangeables, often used to distinguish human beings from the animals, is the desire and ability to relate to past heritage, to tie this heritage into the present, and to extend the present into the future.

It is easy to say, "live in the present," but for many reasons, it's almost impossible to do. One of the reasons is that the things we live with today were created in the past, and today's creations will probably exist in the future. The architects of today's skyscrapers are telling us and future generations what our society's values are. Creative people often extend their statement of life into the future. The ac-

Interior – Guggenheim Museum

ceptance of their work by the public is a reinforcement that the artist is sensitive to the times and has interpreted life appropriately for them too.

From our paintings, our music, our literature, and our buildings, the message of how we searched for and interpreted the meaning of our lives in our time will be read again and again by future generations.

The United Nations Building reaches toward the heavens in search of peace.

BIBLIOGRAPHY

Allen, E.L. *From Plato to Nietzsc*he, British Title: Guide Book to Western Thought, Connecticut: Fawcett Publications, 1964.

Baumgart, Fritz, *A History of Architectural Styles*, New York: Praeger Publishers, 1969.

Beatty and Johnson, Eds. *Heritage of Western Civilization*, 2nd ed. New Jersey: Printice Hall. 1966.

Beckett, Samuel, *Waiting for Godot,* New York: Grove Press, 1954.

Bourne, Russell. Series Editor, *Great Ages of Man*, "Cradle of *Civilization*," "*Ancient Egypt*," "*Classical Greece*," "*Imperial Rome*," "*Renaissance*," New York: Time Inc., 1965.

Bronowski, J., *The Ascent of Man,* Boston, Toronto: Little, Brown and Company, 1973.

Canby, C., Ed. *The Epic of Man*, New York: Time Inc., 1961.

Clark, Kenneth, *Civilization*, New York, 1968.

Cranson, Maurice, Ed. *Locke on Politics, Religion, and Education*, New York: Collier-MacMillan, Ltd., 1965.

deBary, William, Ed. *The Buddhist Tradition in India, China, and Japan*, New York: Vintage Books, 1969.

Durant, Will. *Our Oriental Heritage*, New York: Simon & Schuster, 1935.

Easton, S.Boyd; Konner, Melvin; Shostak, Majorie;*The Paleolithic Prescription*, New York: Harper & Row, 1987.

Gardner, Helen, *Art Through the Ages*, ed. de la Croix & Tansey, 5th edition, New York: Harcourt Brace & World, 1970.

Gibbon, Edward, Ed. Dero Saunders, *The Decline and Fall of the Roman Empire*, (abridged) New York: Viking Press, 1969.

Grunfeld, Frederic, "*The Troubadours,*" Horizon Magazine of the Arts, Summer, 1970.

Grunfeld, Frederic, *Music*, New York: Newsweek Books, 1974.

Heer, Friedrich, *The Medieval World*, Cleveland and New York: World Publishing Company, 1961.

Jacobs, David, *Architecture*, New York: Newsweek Books, 1974.

Janson, H.W., and Kerman, Joseph, *A History of Art and Music,* New Jersey and New York: Prentice-Hall, Inc., and Harry N. Abrams, Inc.

Jaspers, Karl, (Eds. H. Arendt, translater R. Manheim) *The Great Philosophers*, New York: Harcourt, Brace & World, Inc., 1957.

Kaufmann, W. E., *Existentialism from Dostoyevsky to Sartre,* Cleveland and New York: World Publising Co., 1956.

McMullen, Roy, "*The Lascaux Puzzle,*" Horizon Magazine of the Arts, Spring, 1969.

Michener, James, *The Source*, Random House, New York, 1965.

Morton, Robert, Series Ed., *Time-Life Library of Art*, New York: Time Inc., 1969.

O'Connell, Robert L., *Of Arms and Men, A History of War, Weapons and Aggression.* New

York, Oxford: Oxford University Press, 1989.

Pignatti, Terisio, *Painting Through the Eighteenth Century,* New York: Newsweek Books, 1974.

Rouse, W.H.D., translator, *Great Dialogues of Plato*, New York: New American Library (Mentor), 1956

Salzman, Eric, *Twentieth-Century Music: An Introduction,* New Jersey: Prentice-Hall, Inc., 1967.

Severy, Merle, Ed., *Great Religions of the World,* National Geographic Society, New York, 1971.

Smith, Huston, *The Religions of Man*, New York: Harper & Row, Perennial Library, 1965.

Thomas, Henry, *Understanding the Great Philosophers*, New York: Doubleday, 1962.

Van Loon, Hendrik, *The Story of Mankind*, New York: Garden City Publishing Co., Inc., 1921.

Wells, H.G., *The Outline of History*, Vols. I & II, New York: The MacMillan Company, 1921.

INDEX